WHOOP! WHOOP!

Whats good Ninja's and Ninjette's!? Normally this is where I put some disclaimer or something about how I have no affiliation with the content of the coloring book in question. But not today—this is a coloring book of and for my own unique and massive family…

The Juggalo Family.

The first coloring page (not the best art in the book, but whatever) is of my own Hatchetman Tattoo.

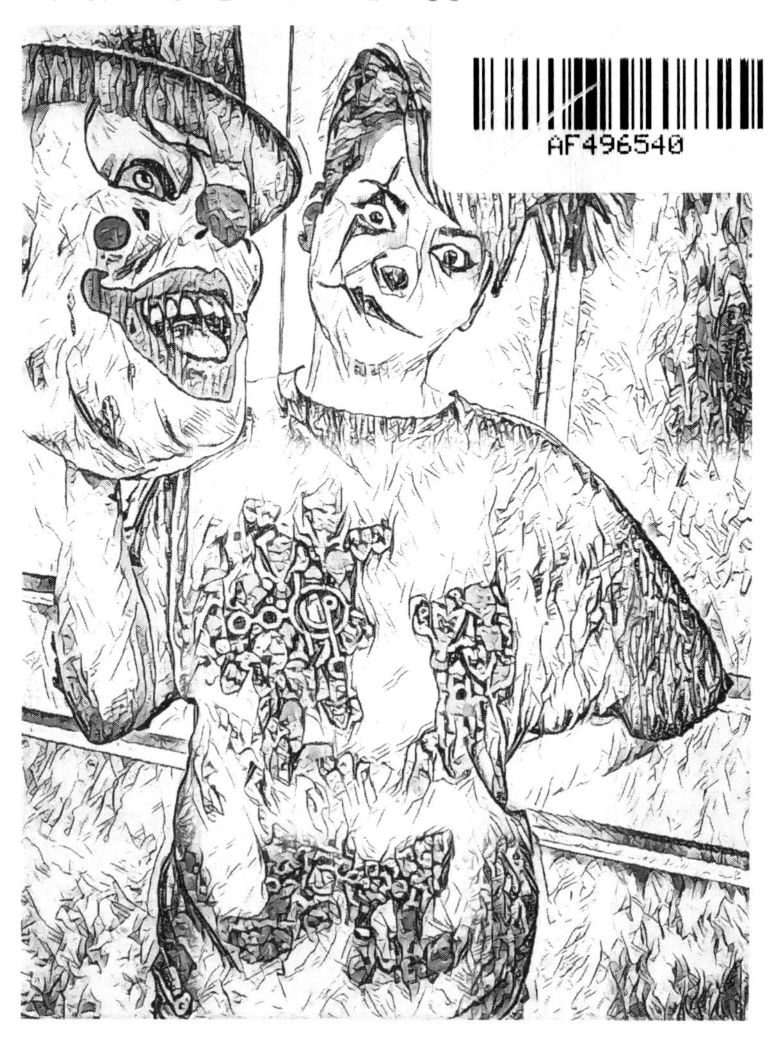

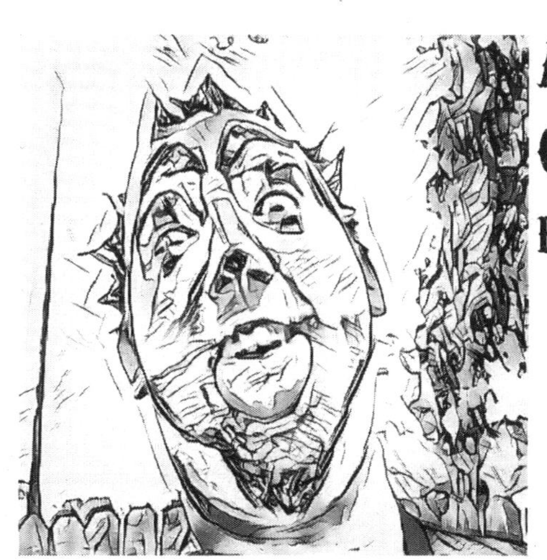

Much Clown Love!

Seriously though, Joe Bruce, dont sue me! Psychopathic Records is his, the family and fellowship that guided me and many others through our turbulent formative years, that is his too, he built that. You taught a generation of misfits and outcasts to be ourselves and gave us something to belong to, and I appreciate that homie I really do.

— J. Wagner

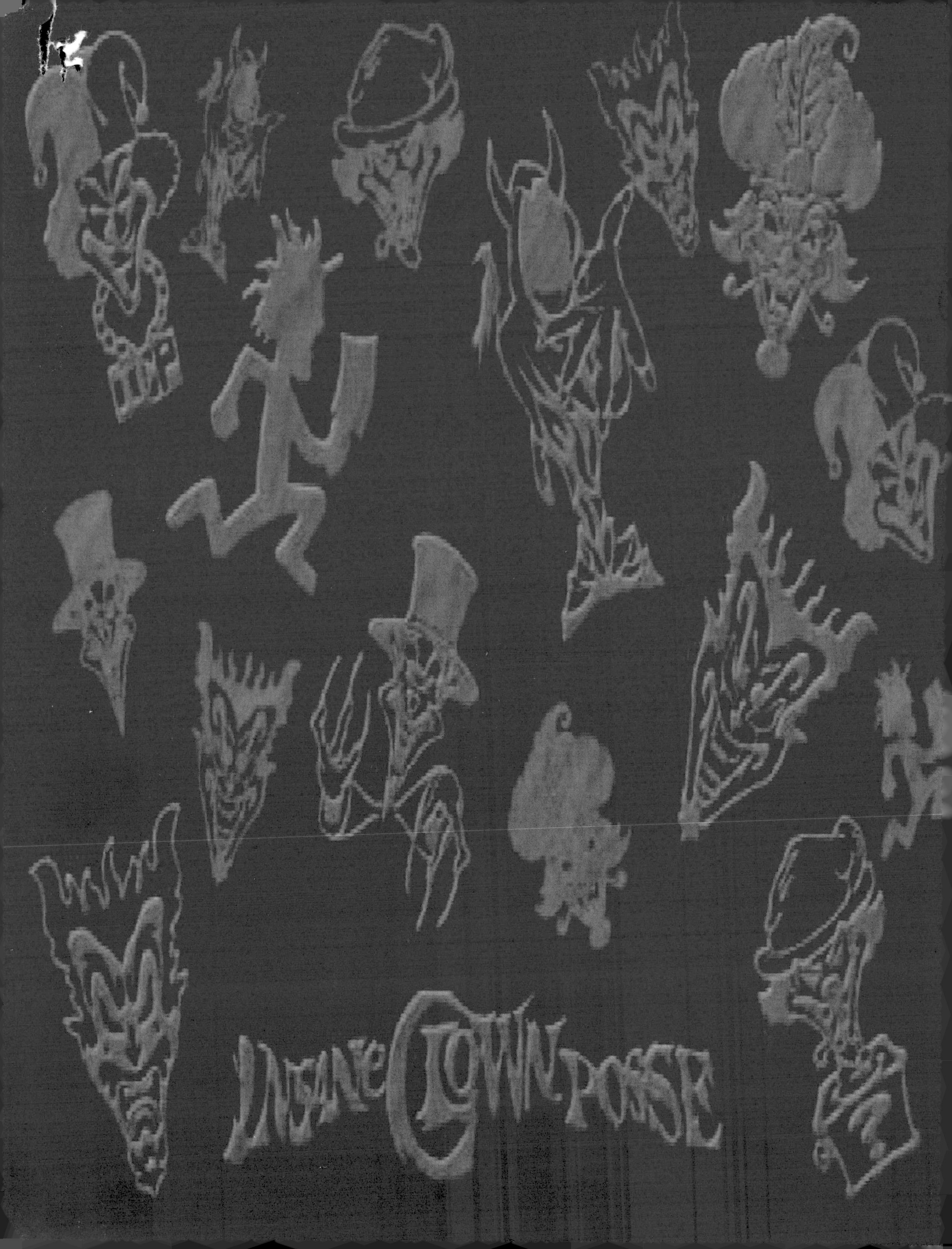

ICP
INSANE CLOWN POSSE

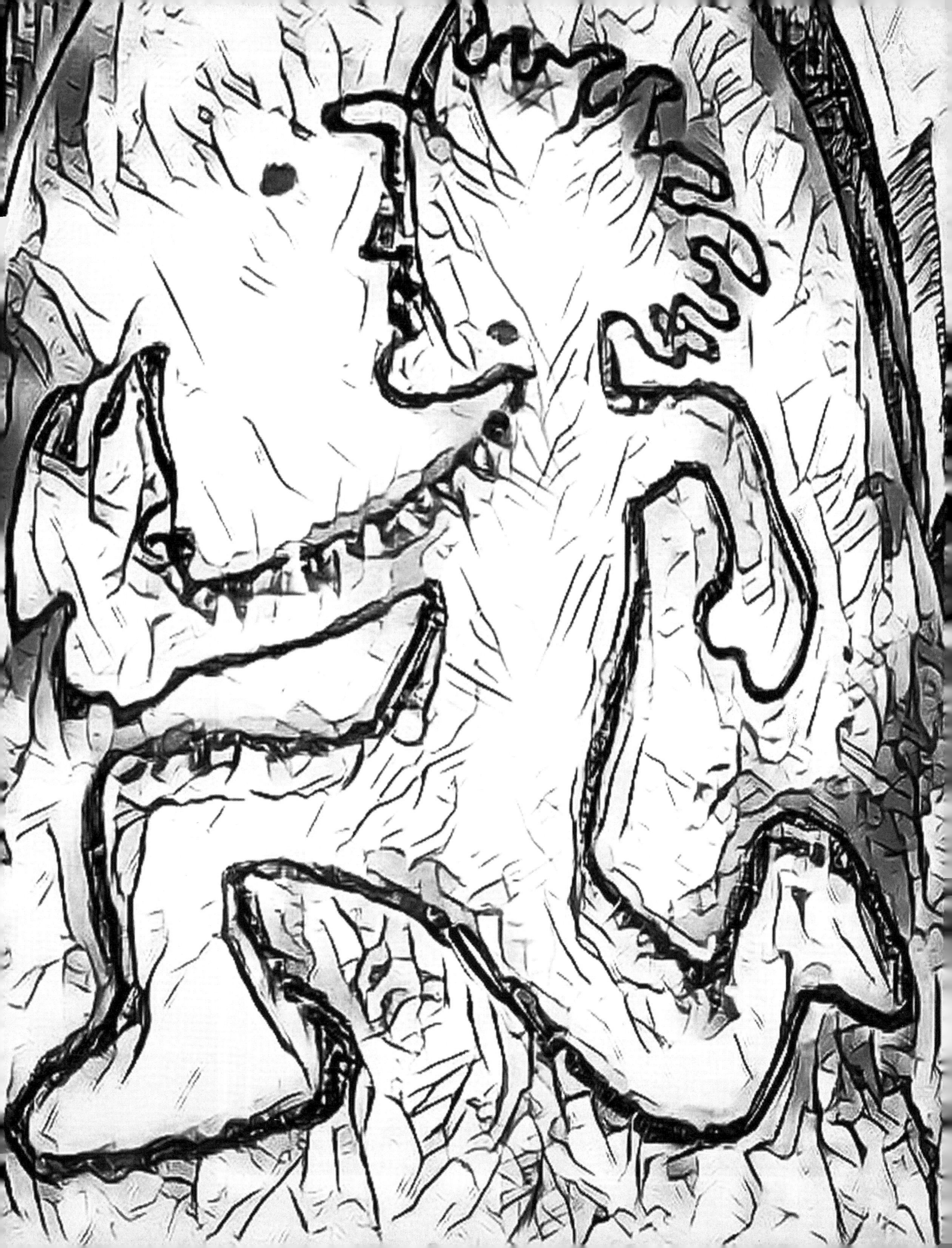

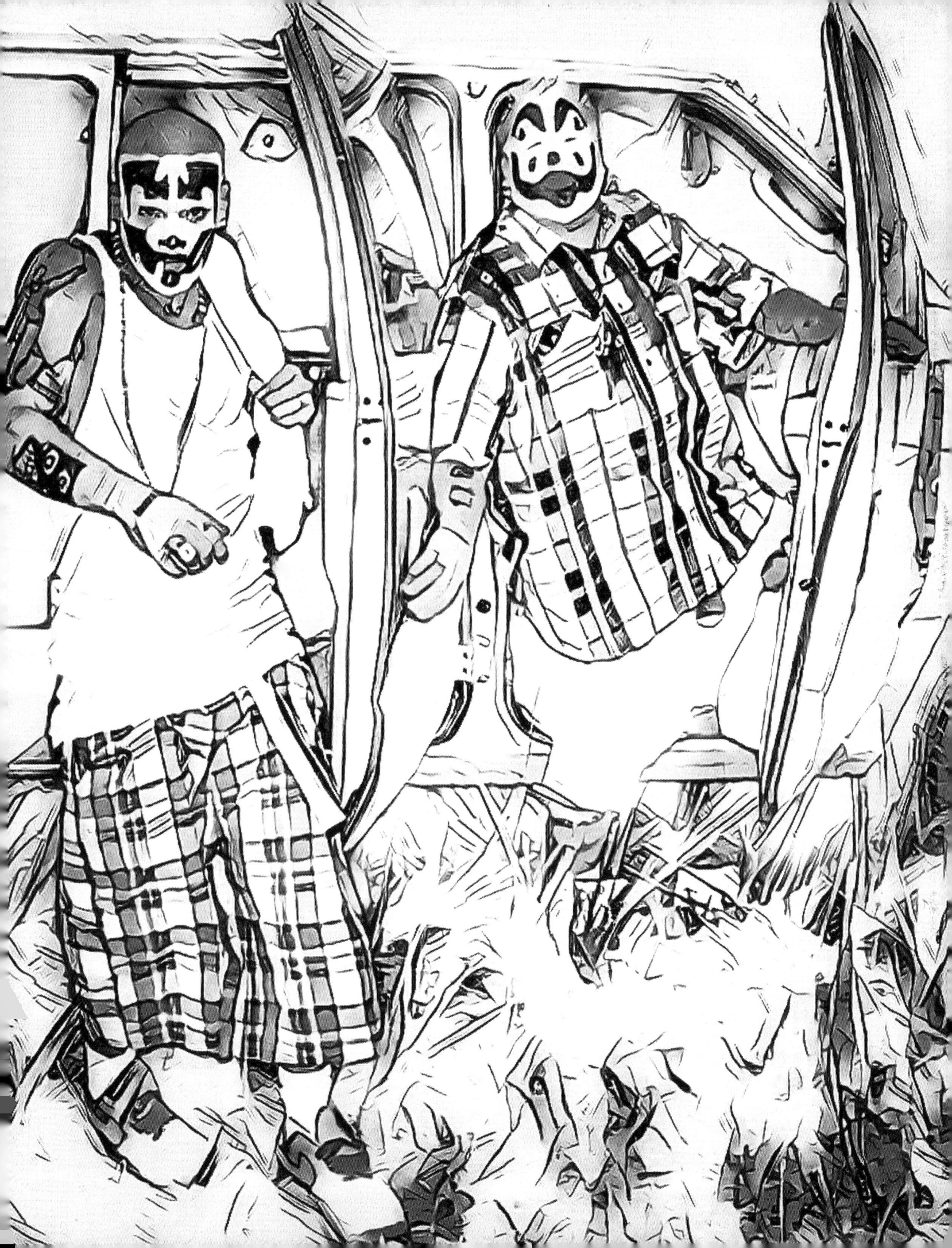

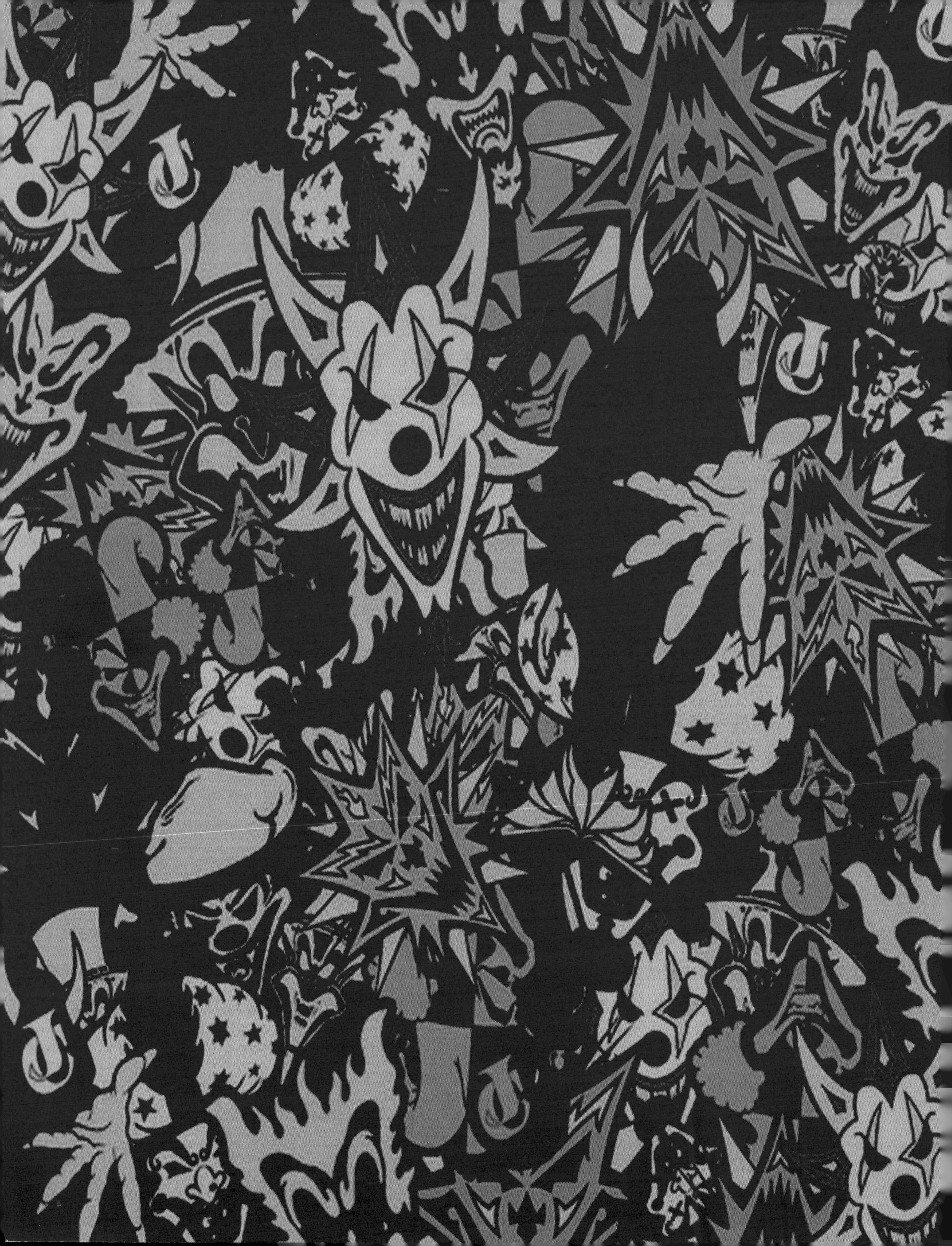

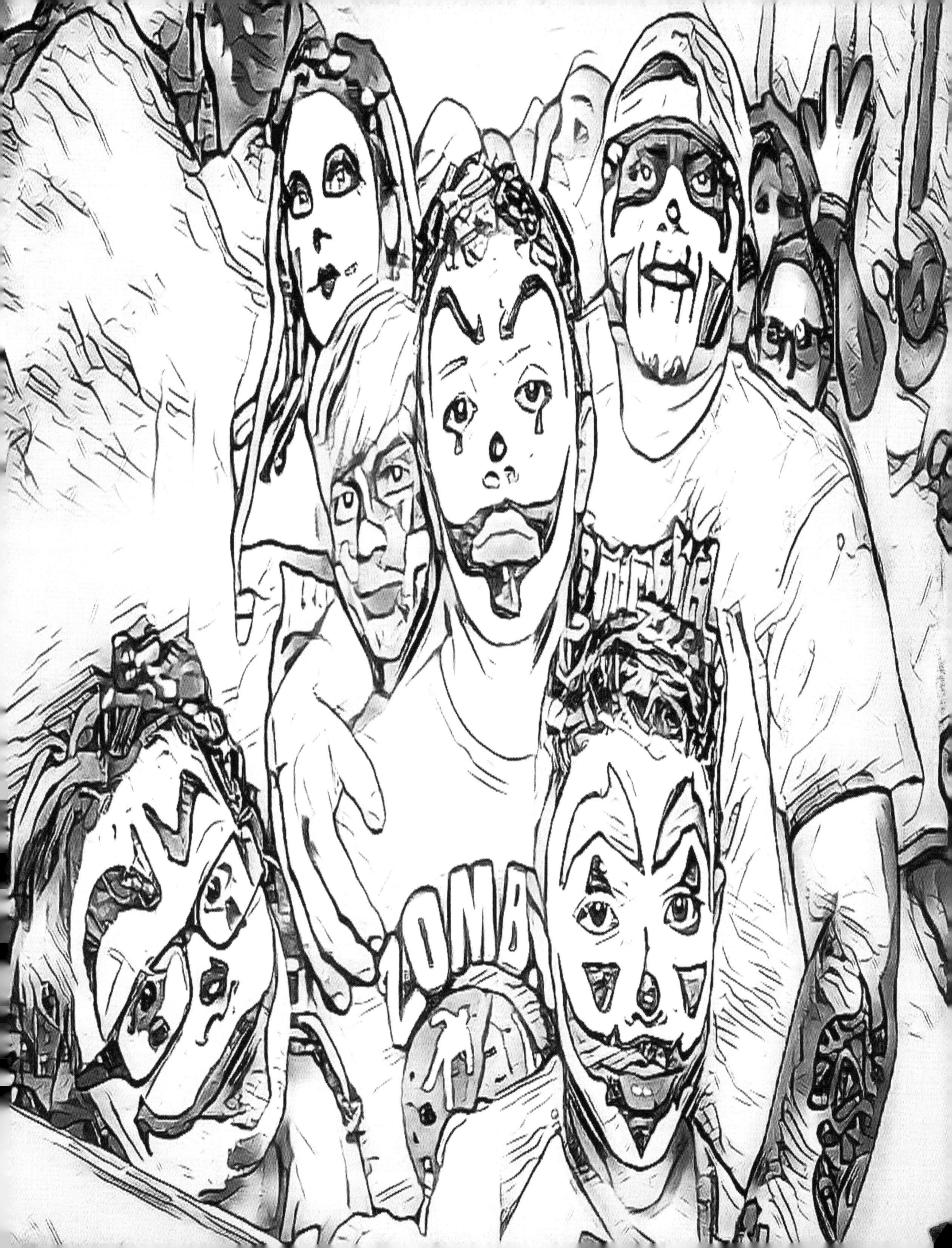
ZOMB

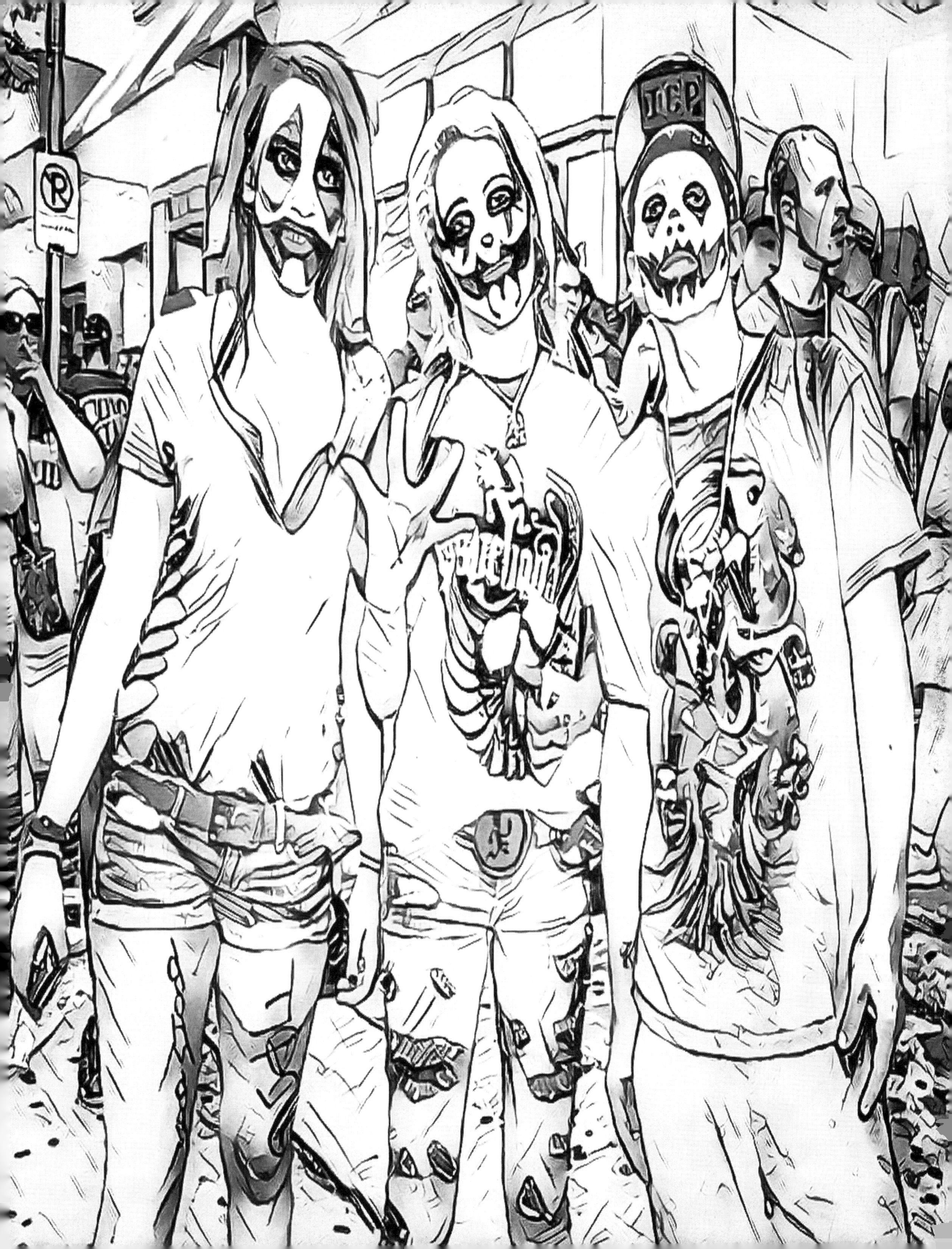

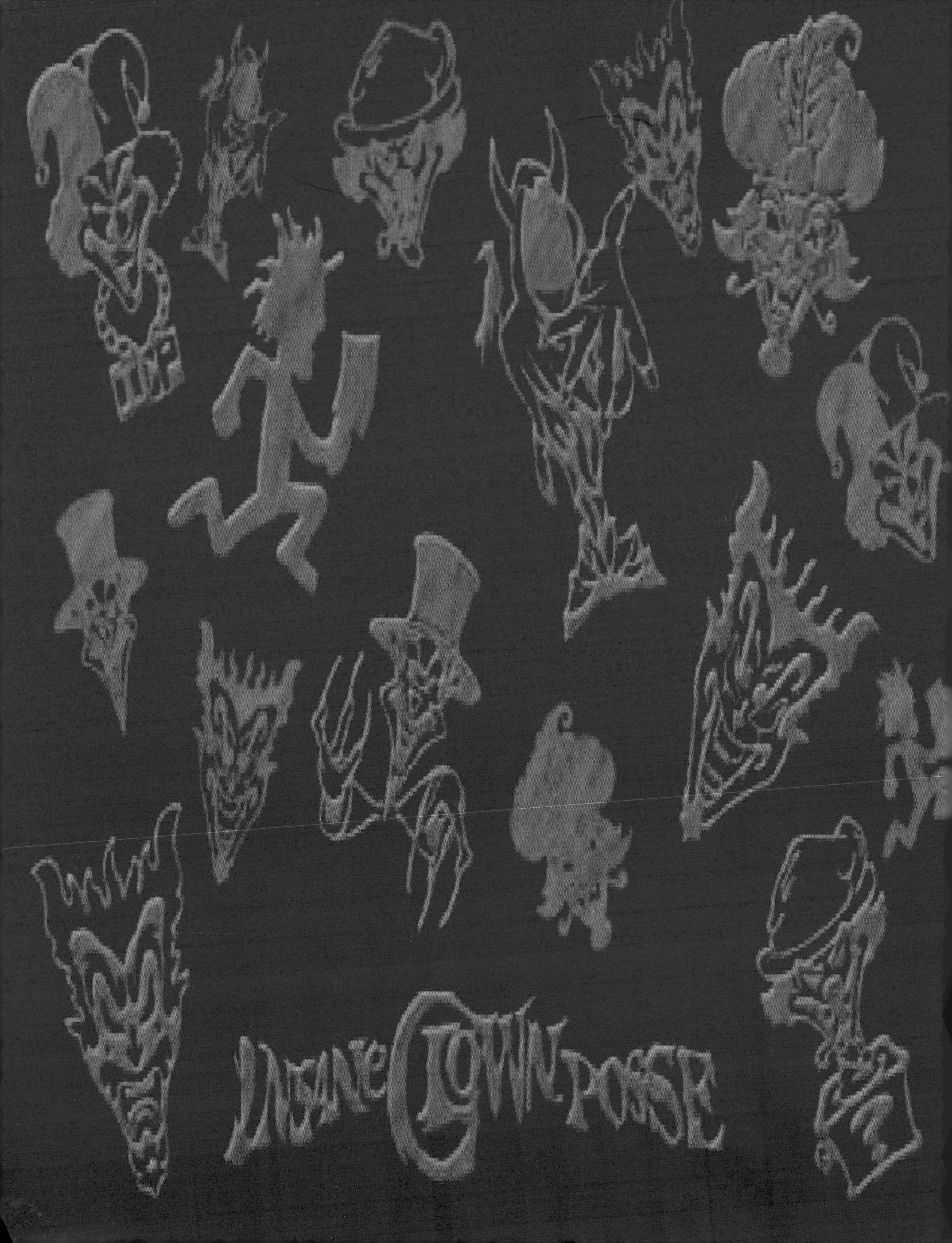

Insane Clown Posse

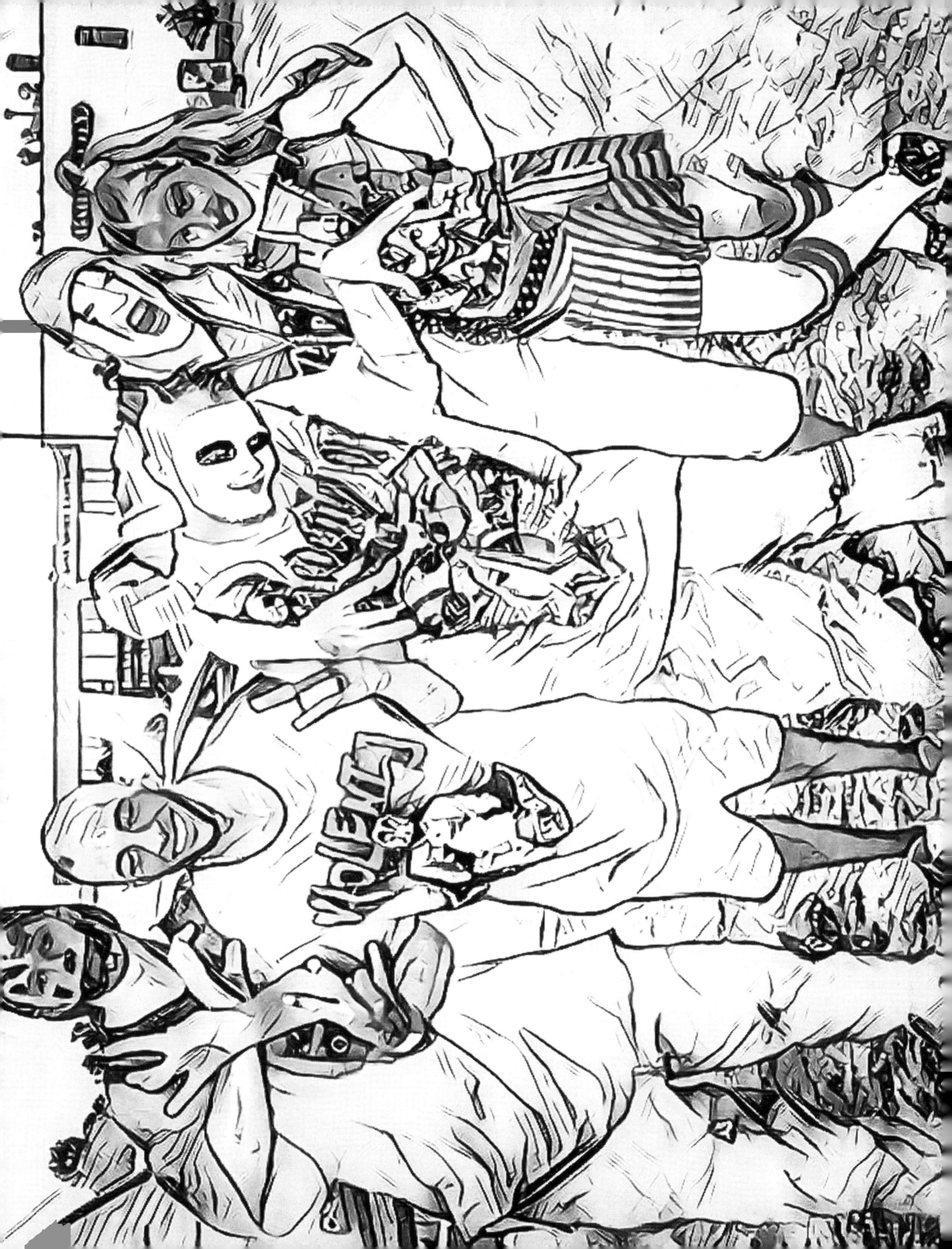

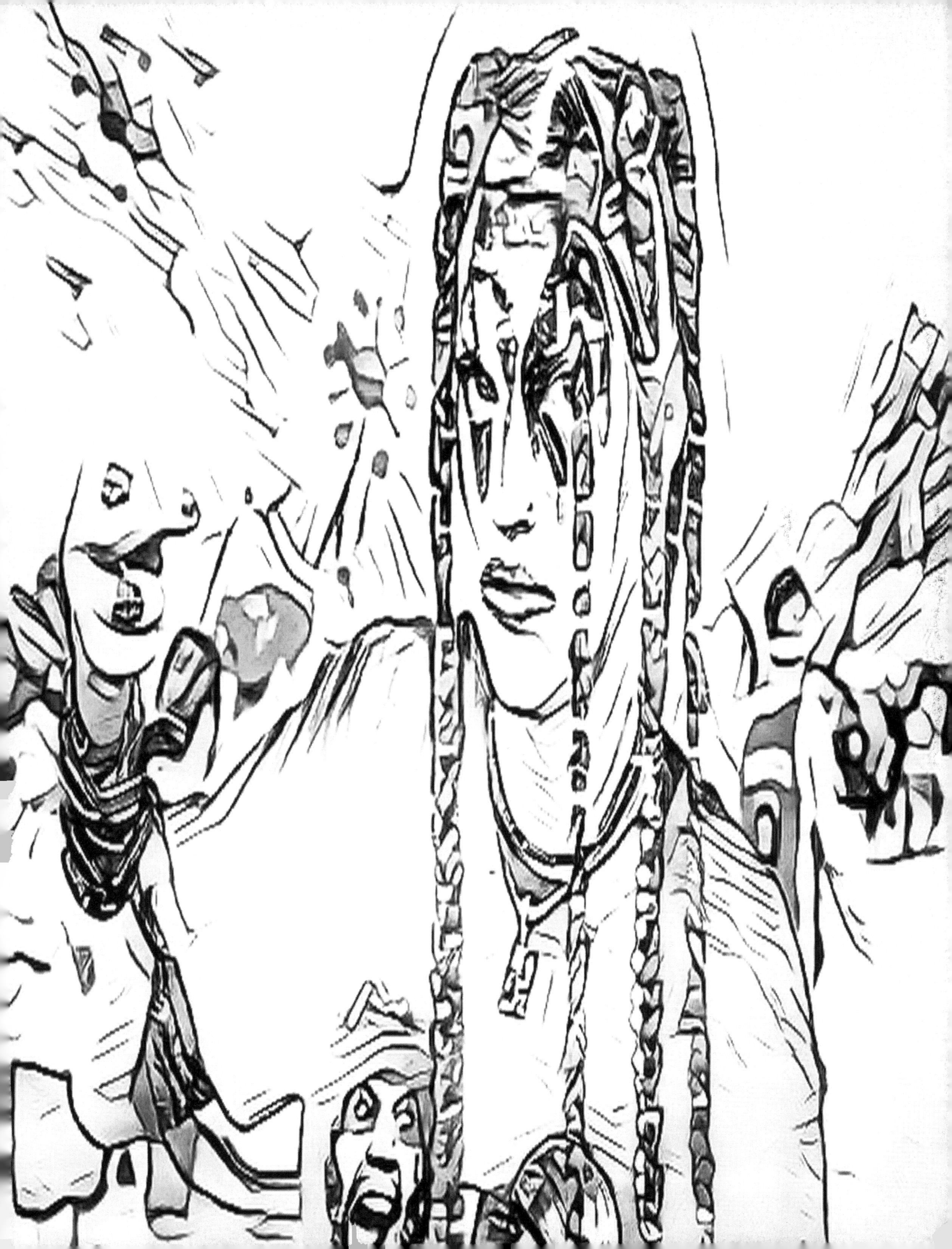

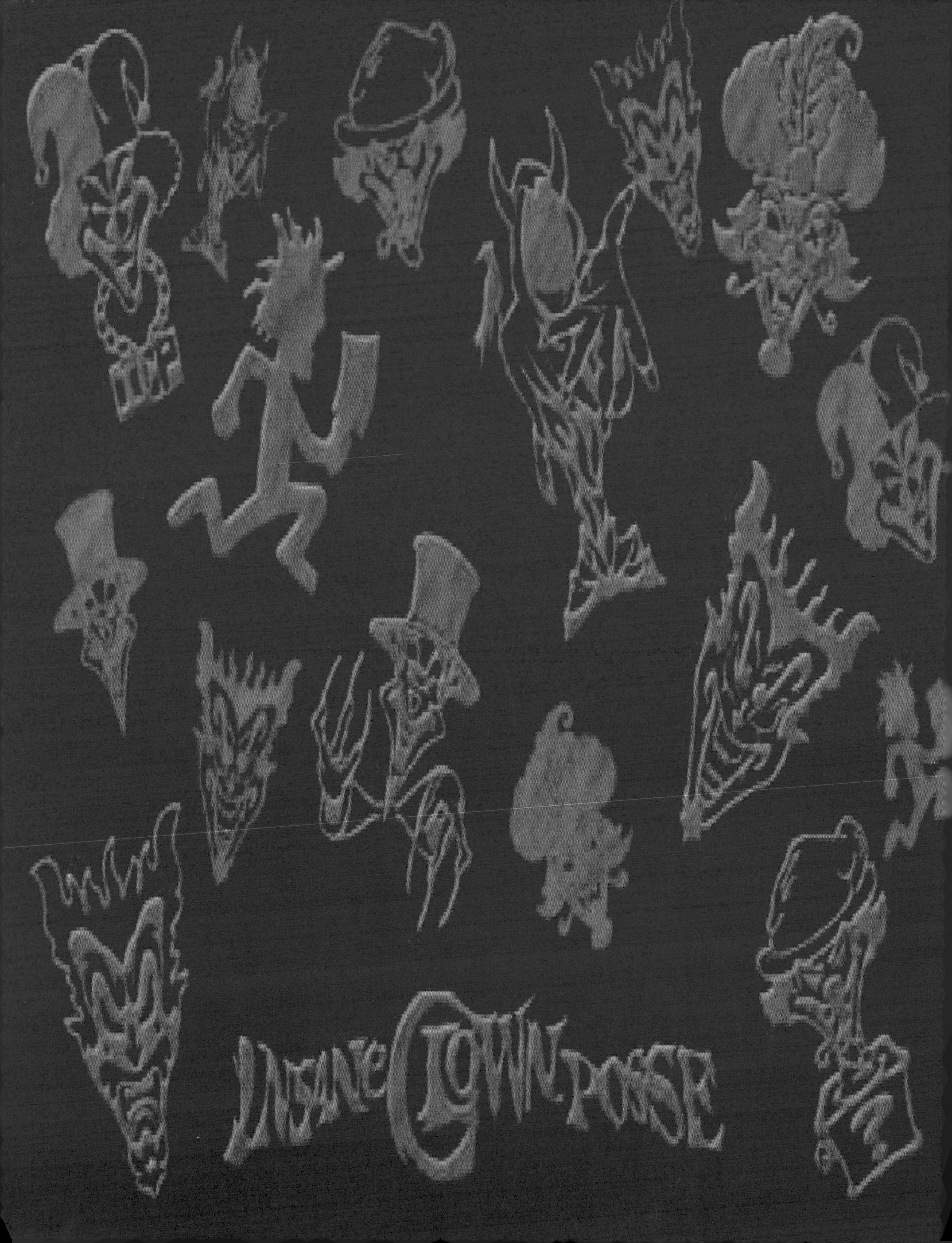

INSANE CLOWN POSSE

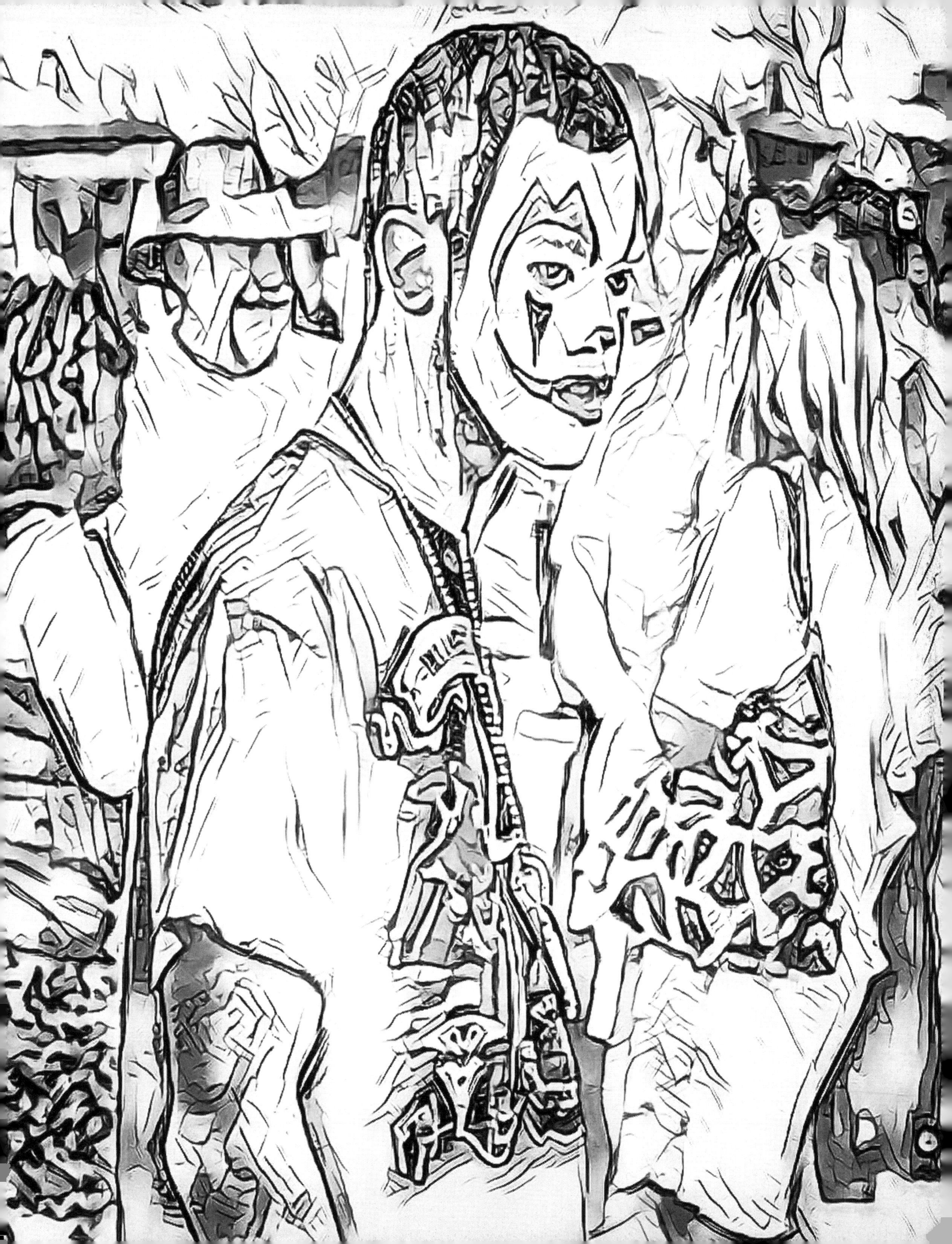

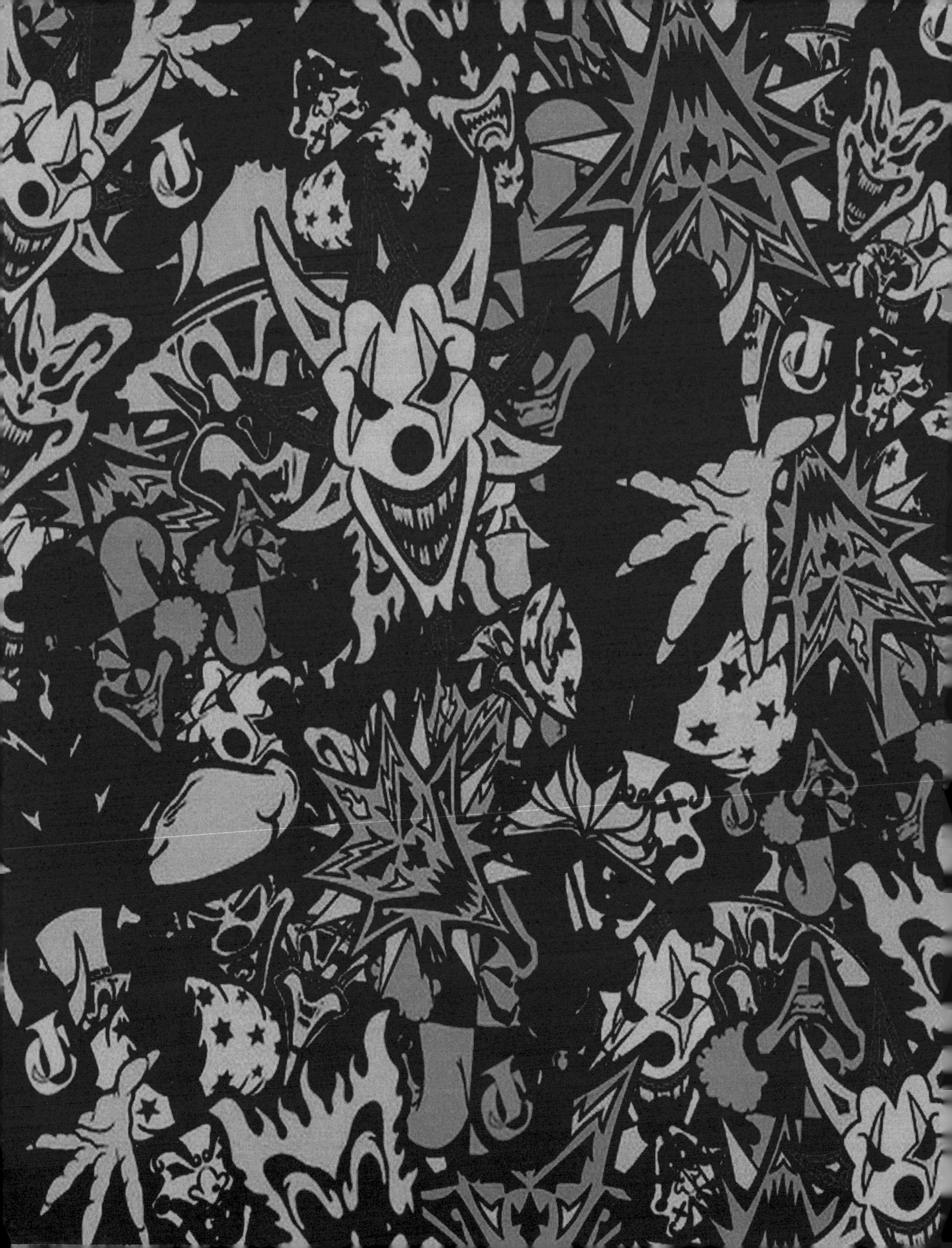

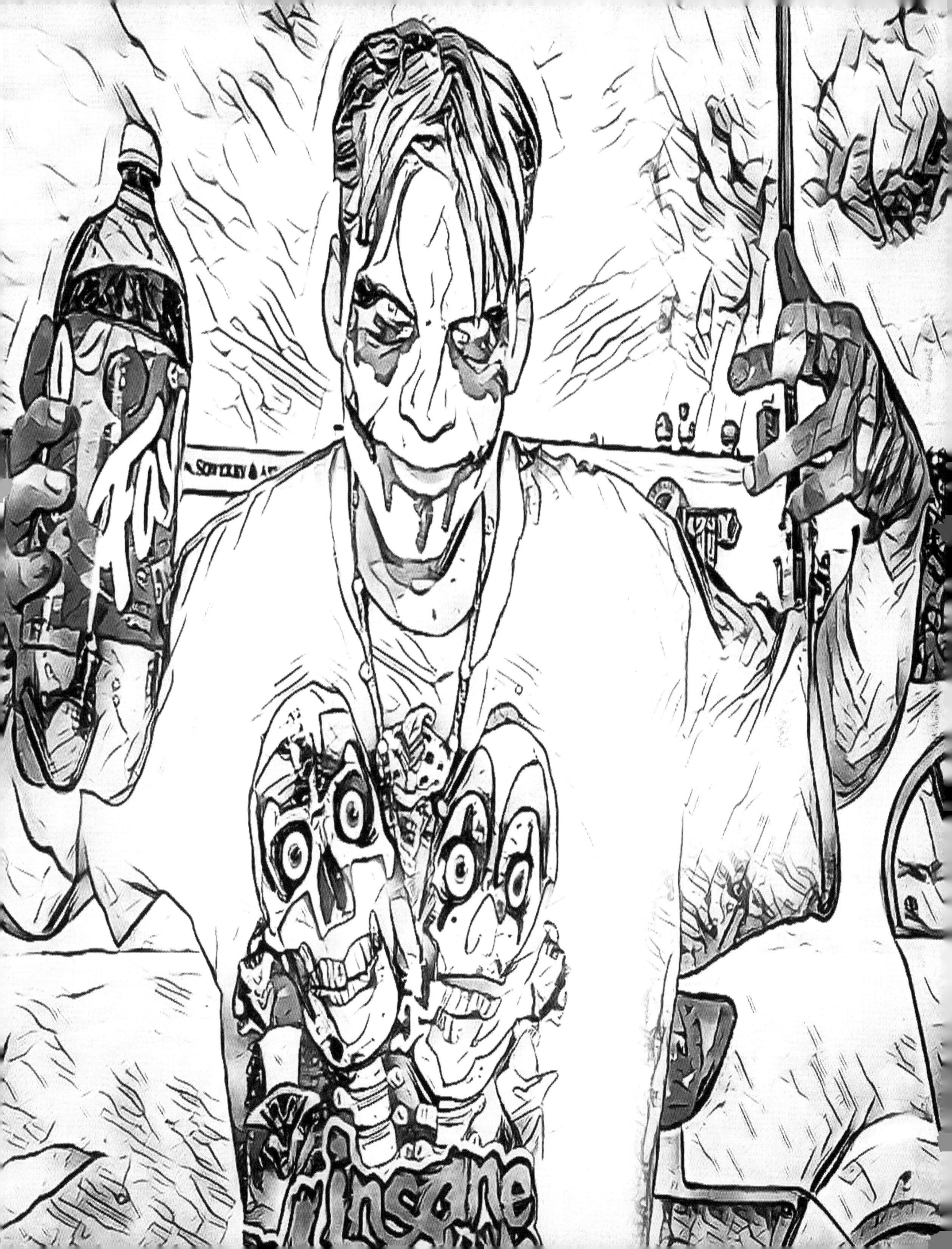
insane

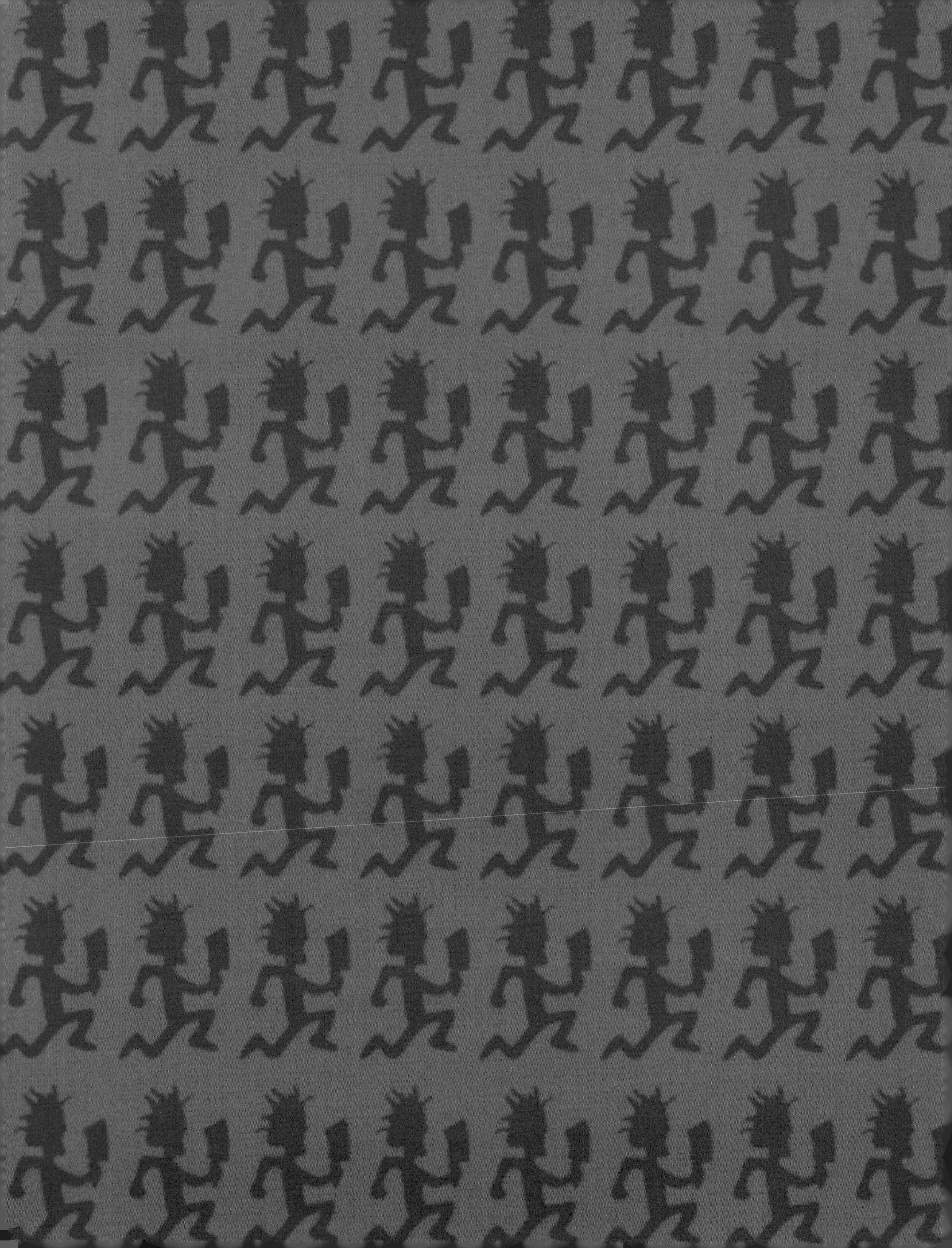

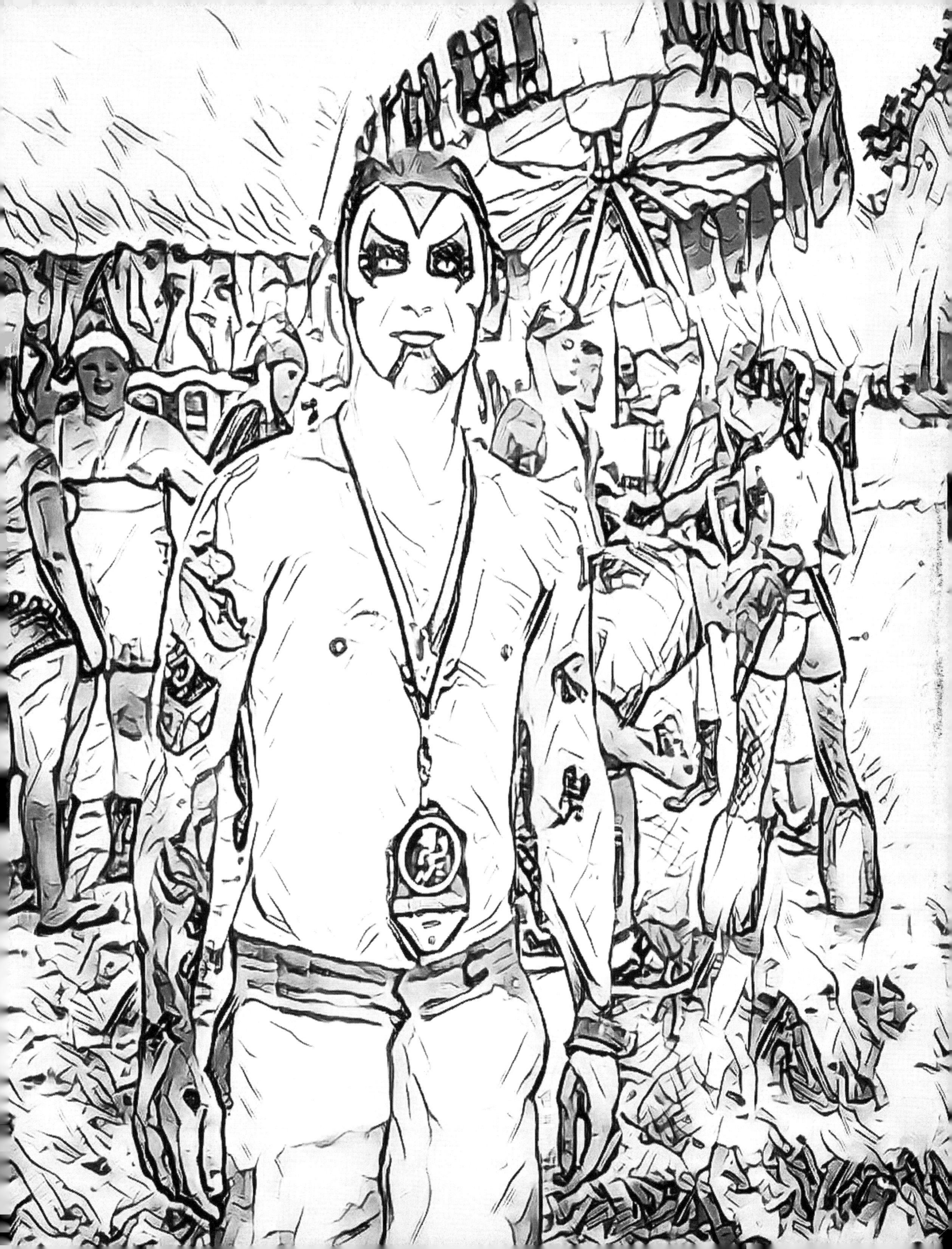

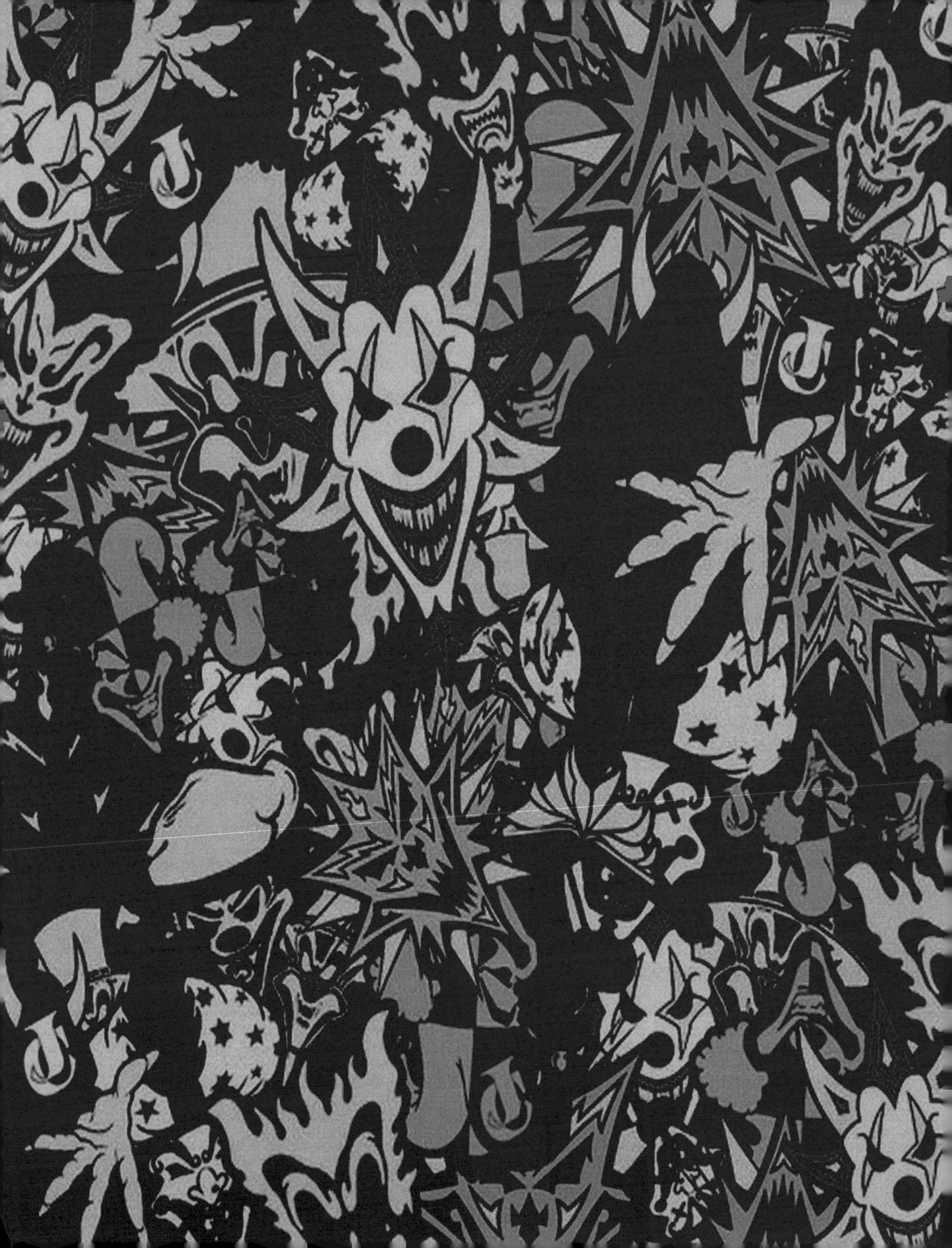

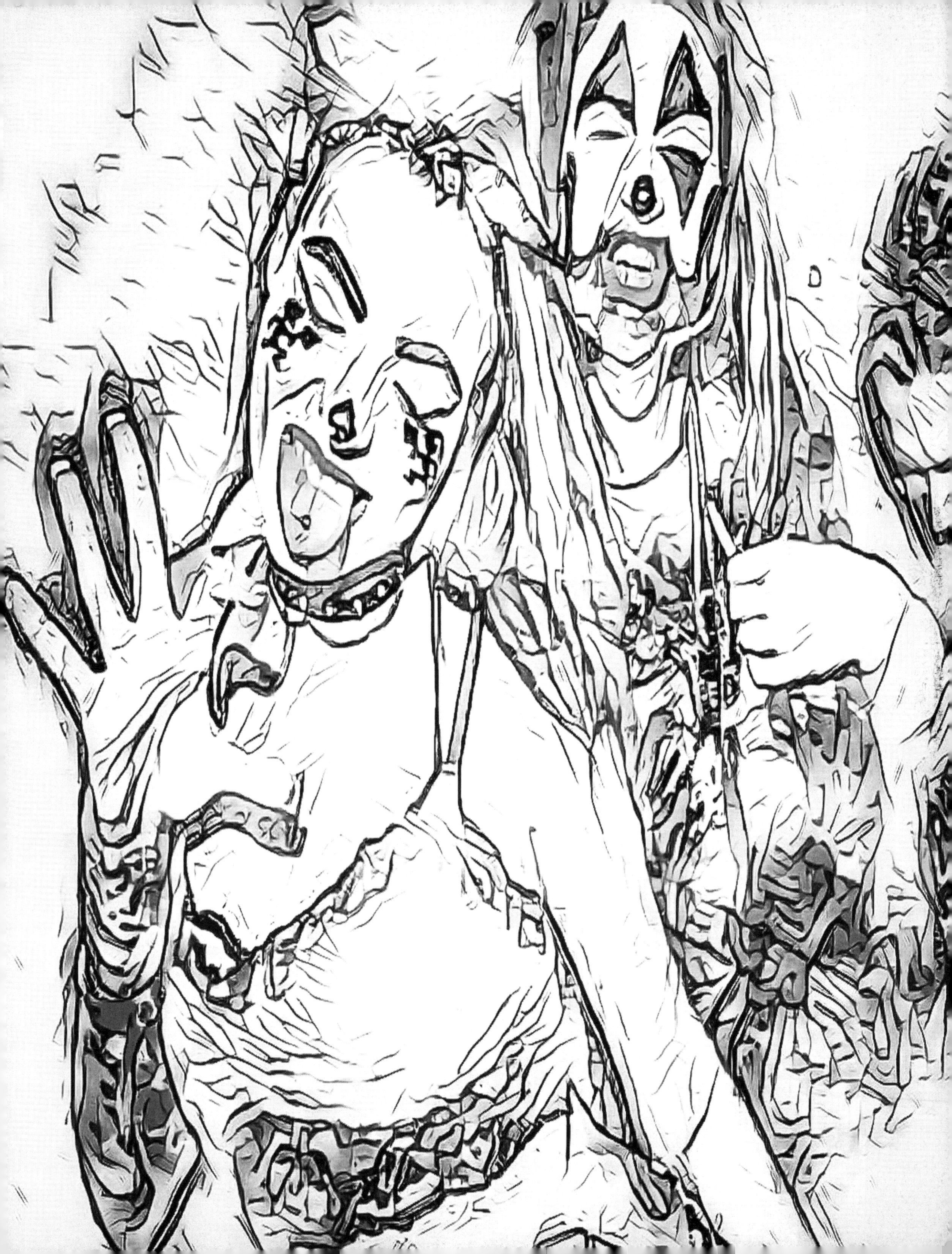

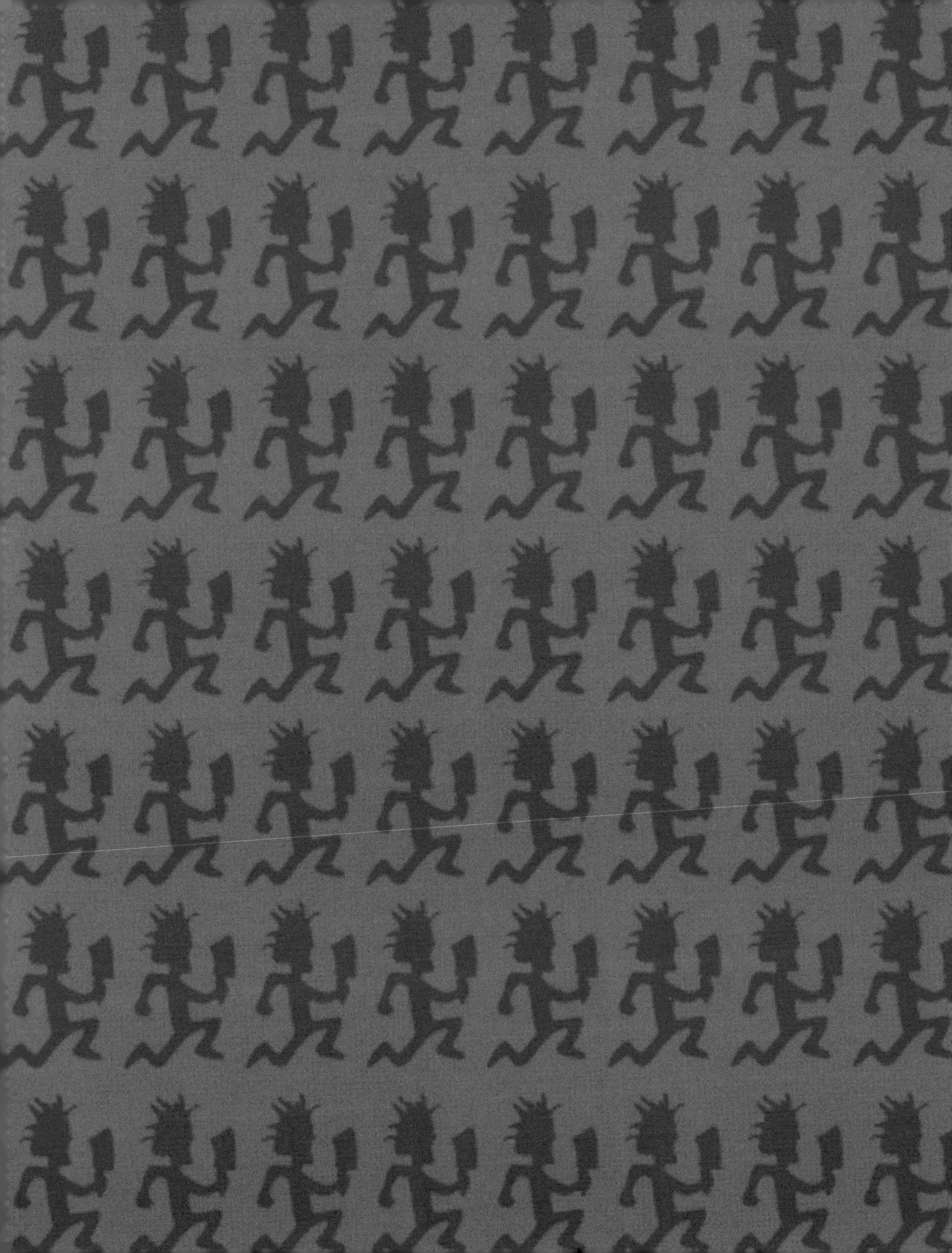

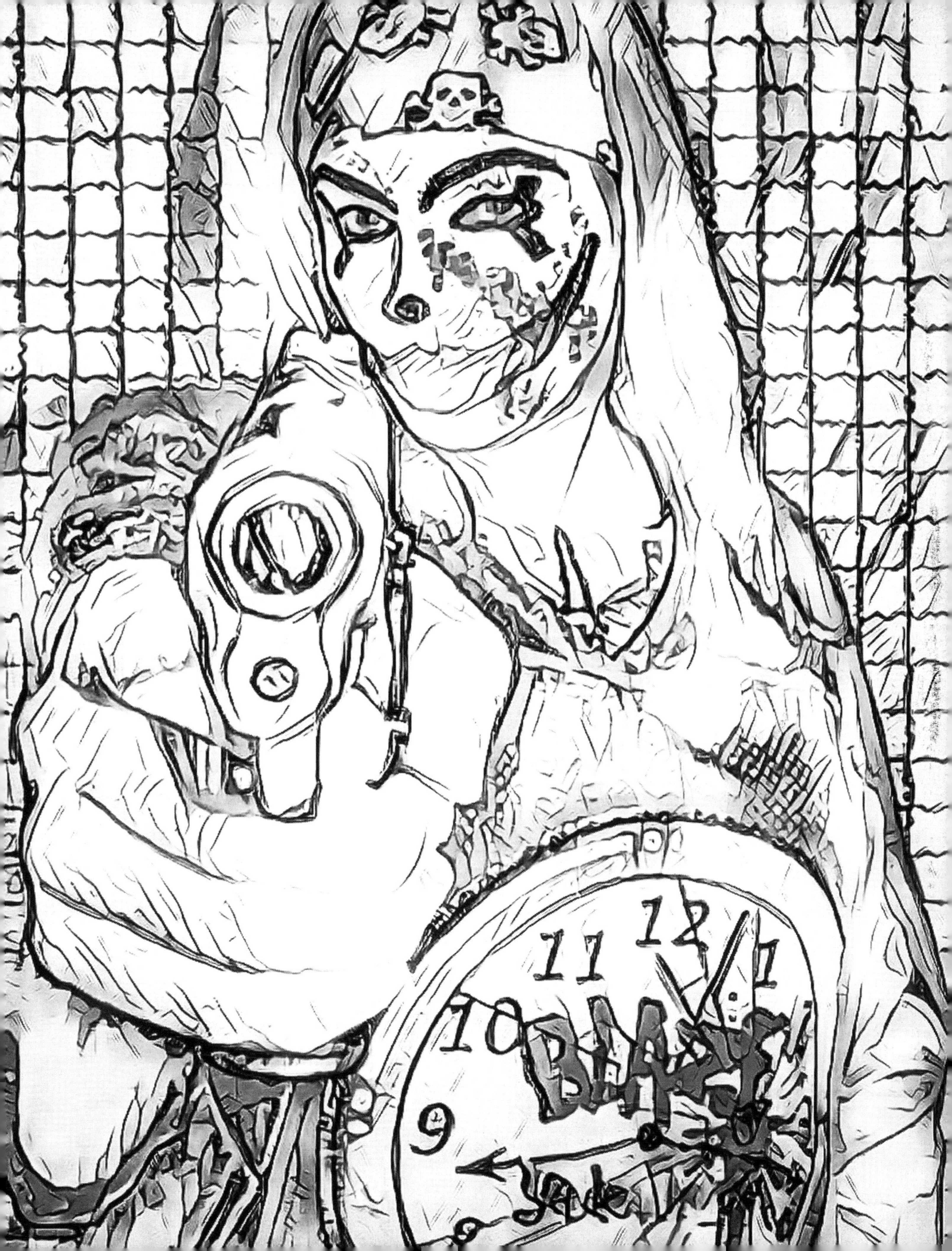

11 12 1
10
9
BLAZE

INSANE CLOWN POSSE

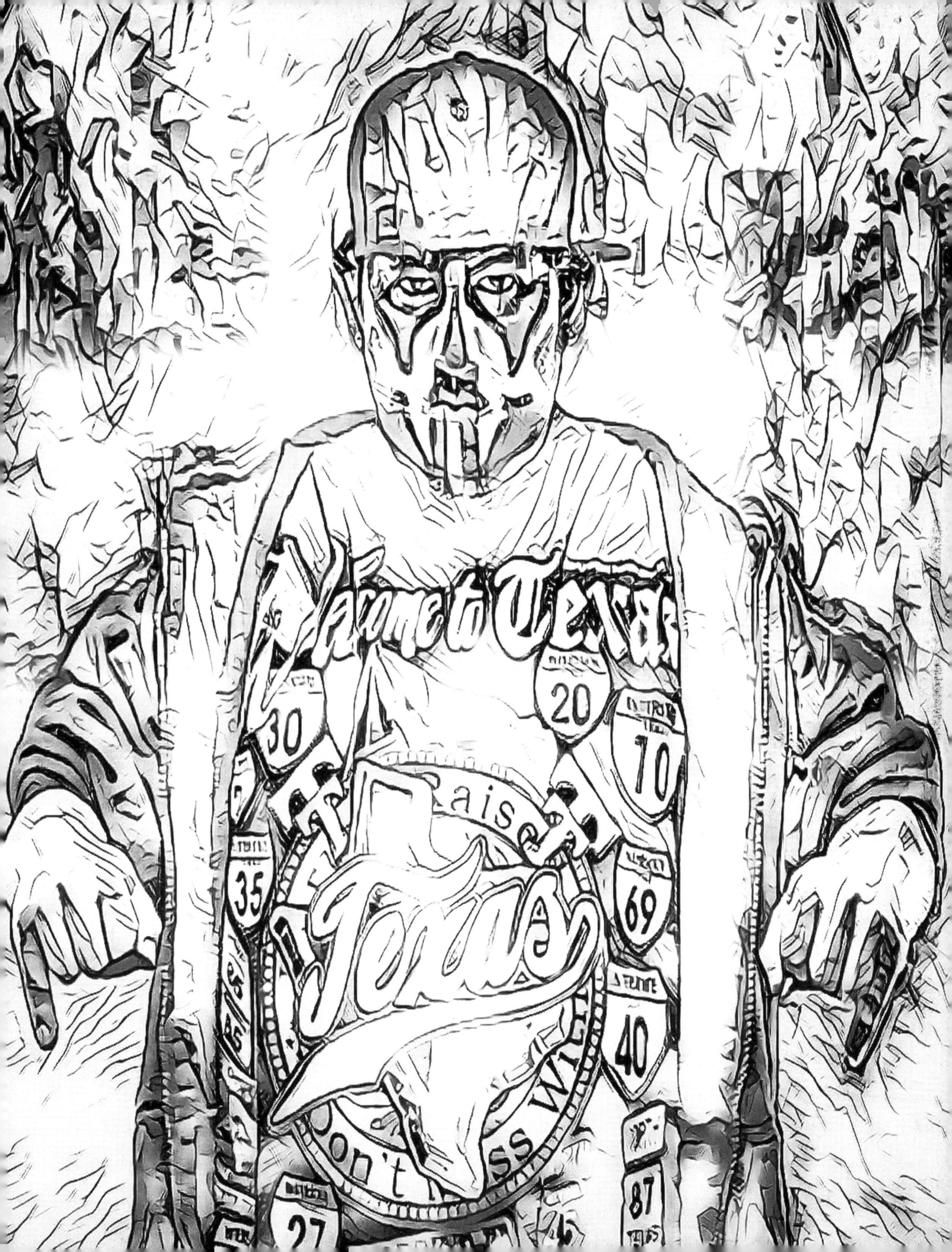

Welcome to Texas
Texas Raised
Texas
Don't Mess With
20
30
10
35
69
40
27
87

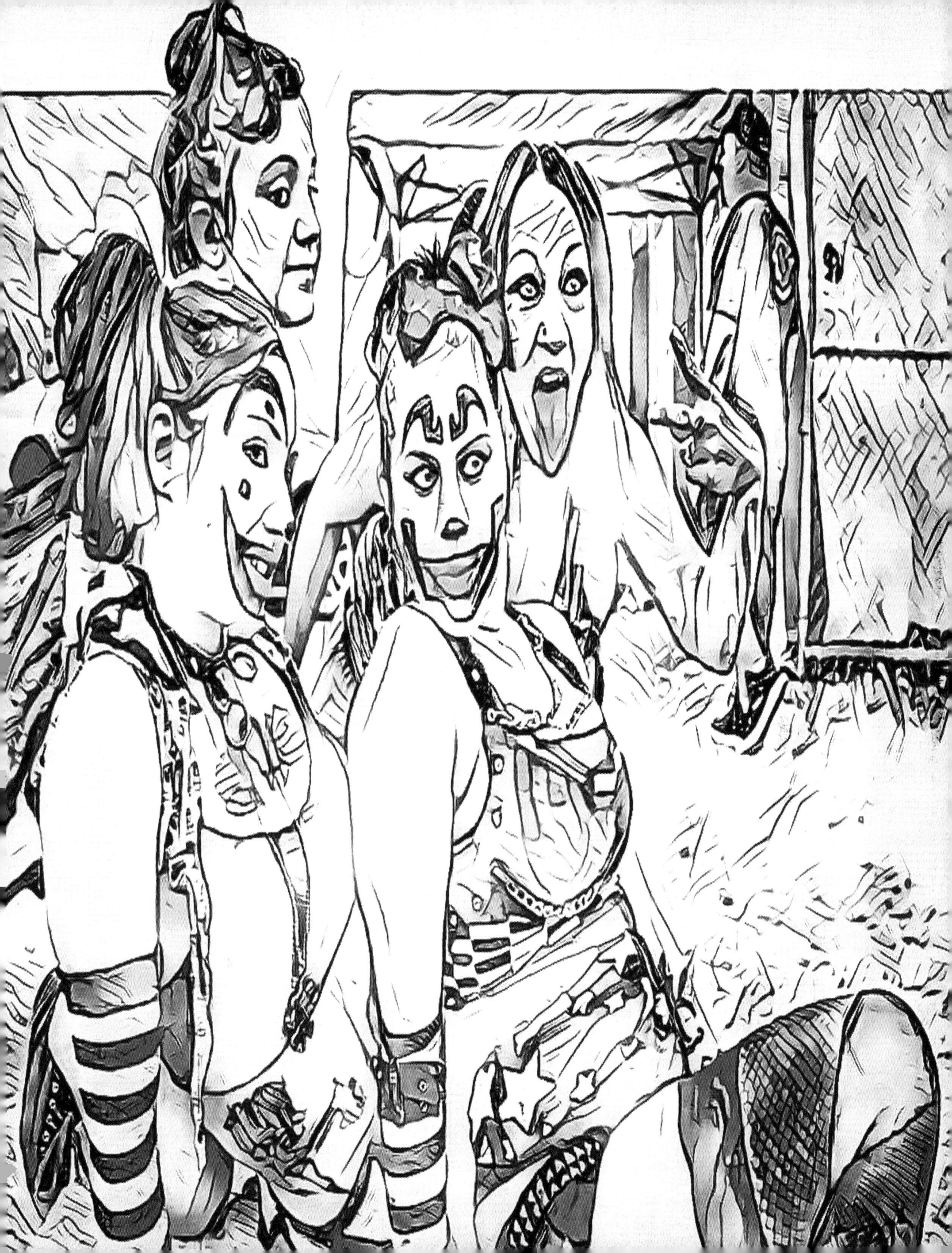

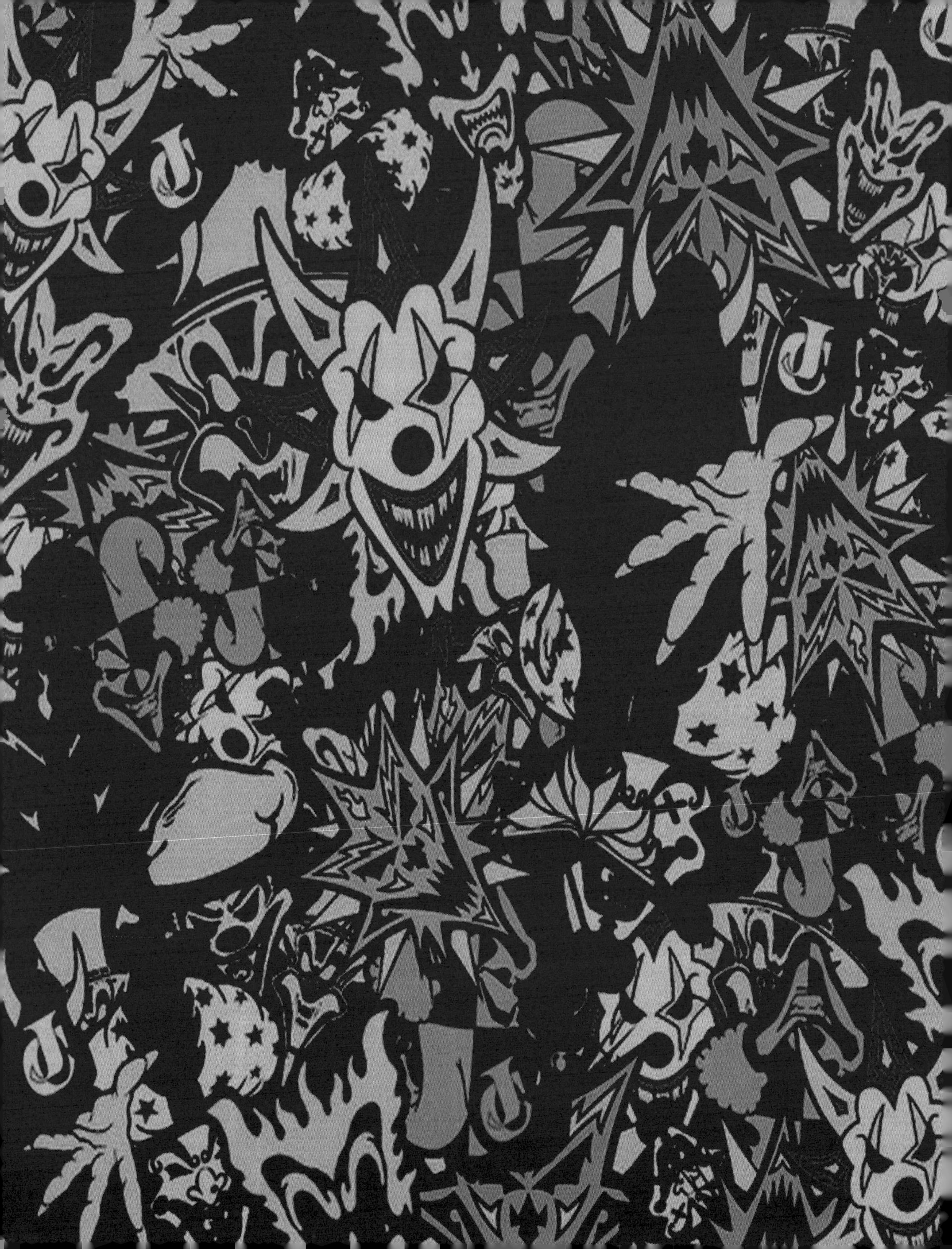

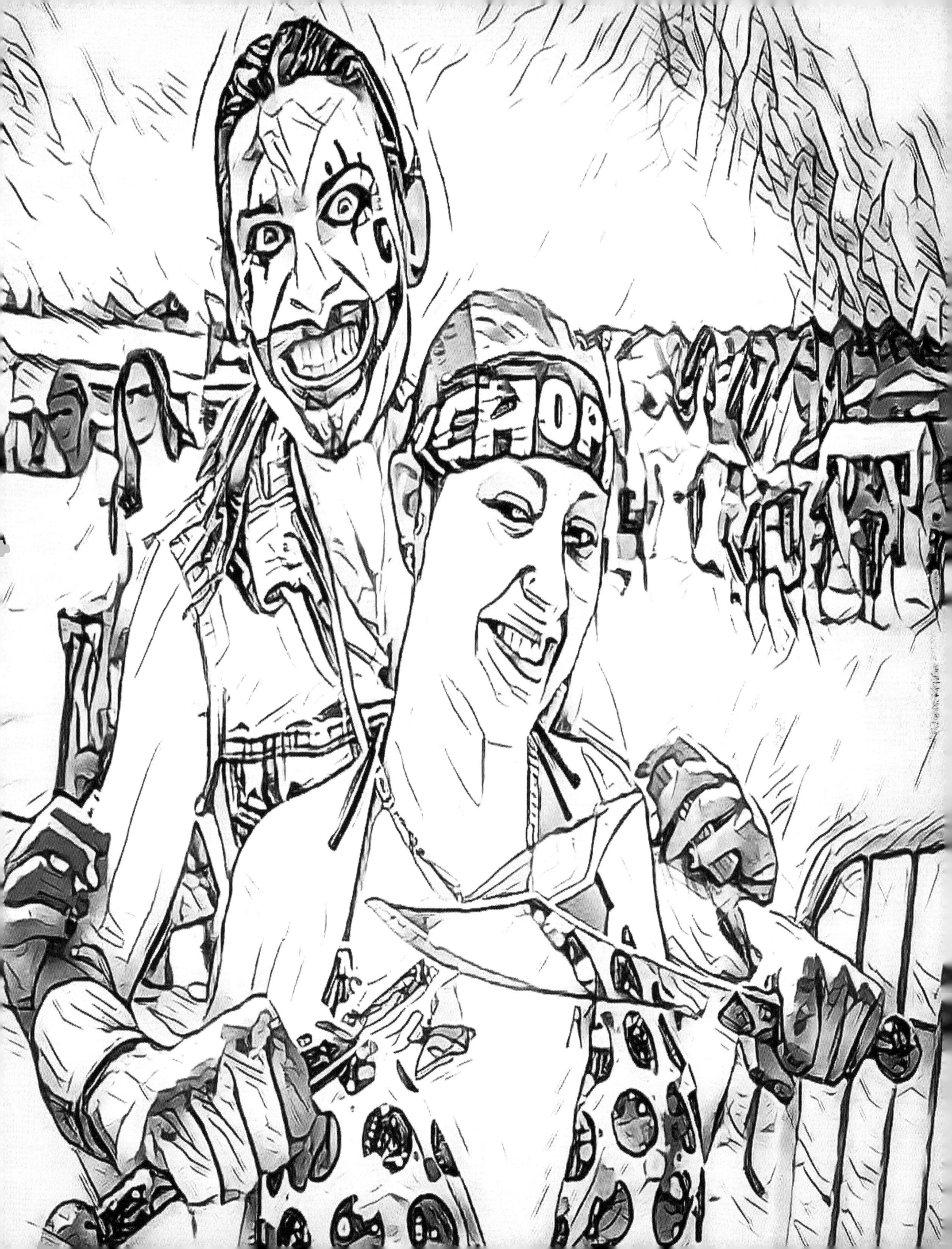
CHOP

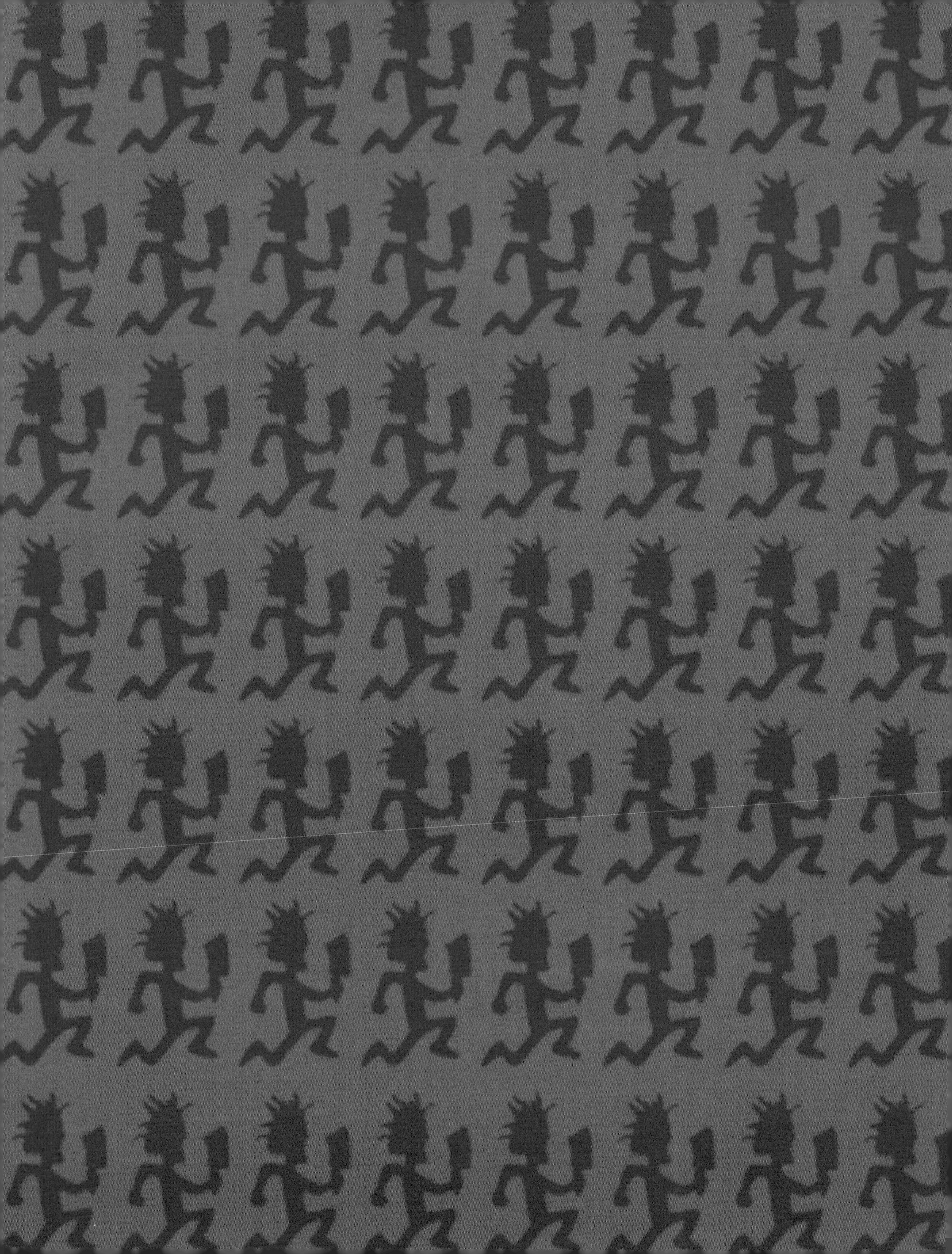

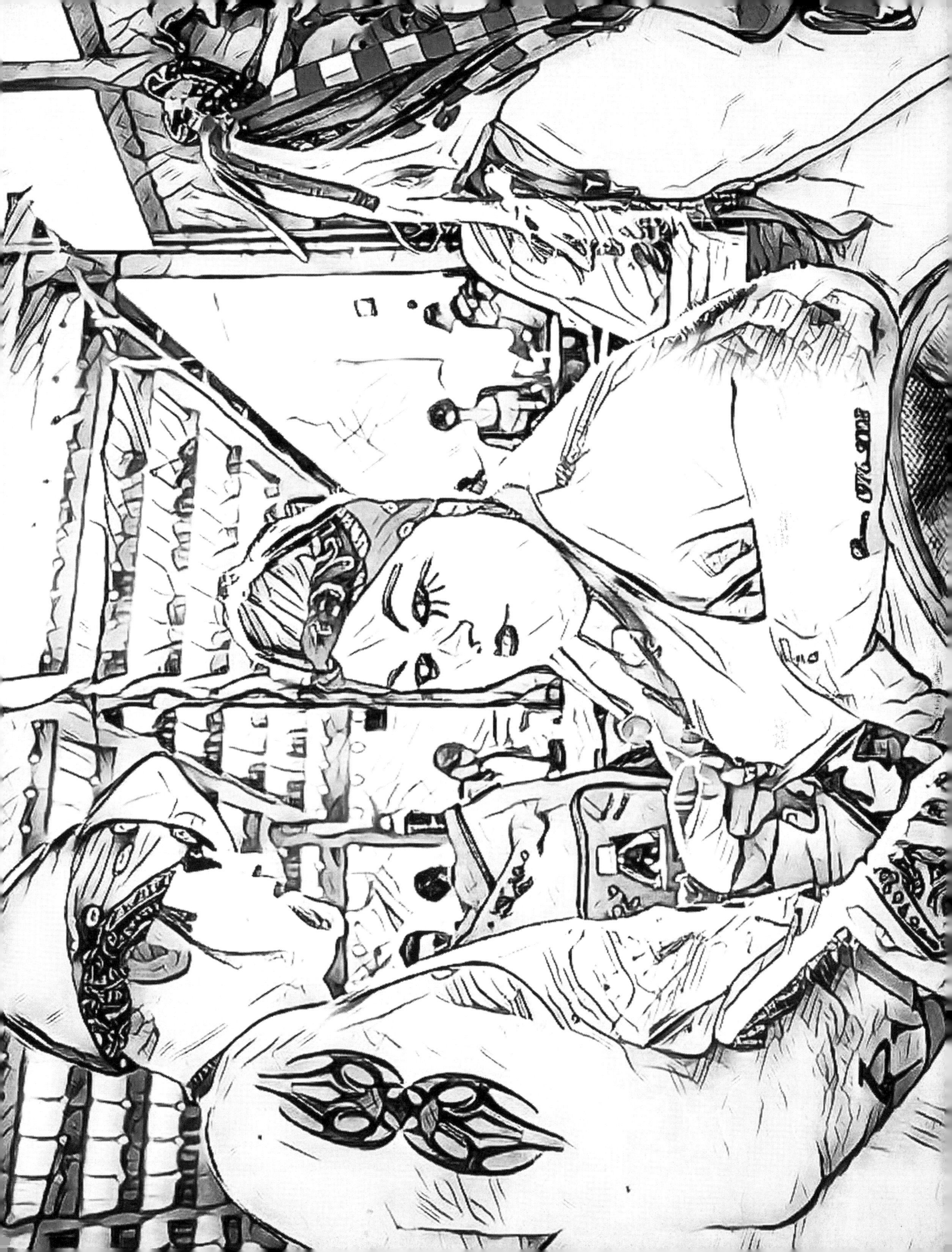

INSANE CLOWN POSSE

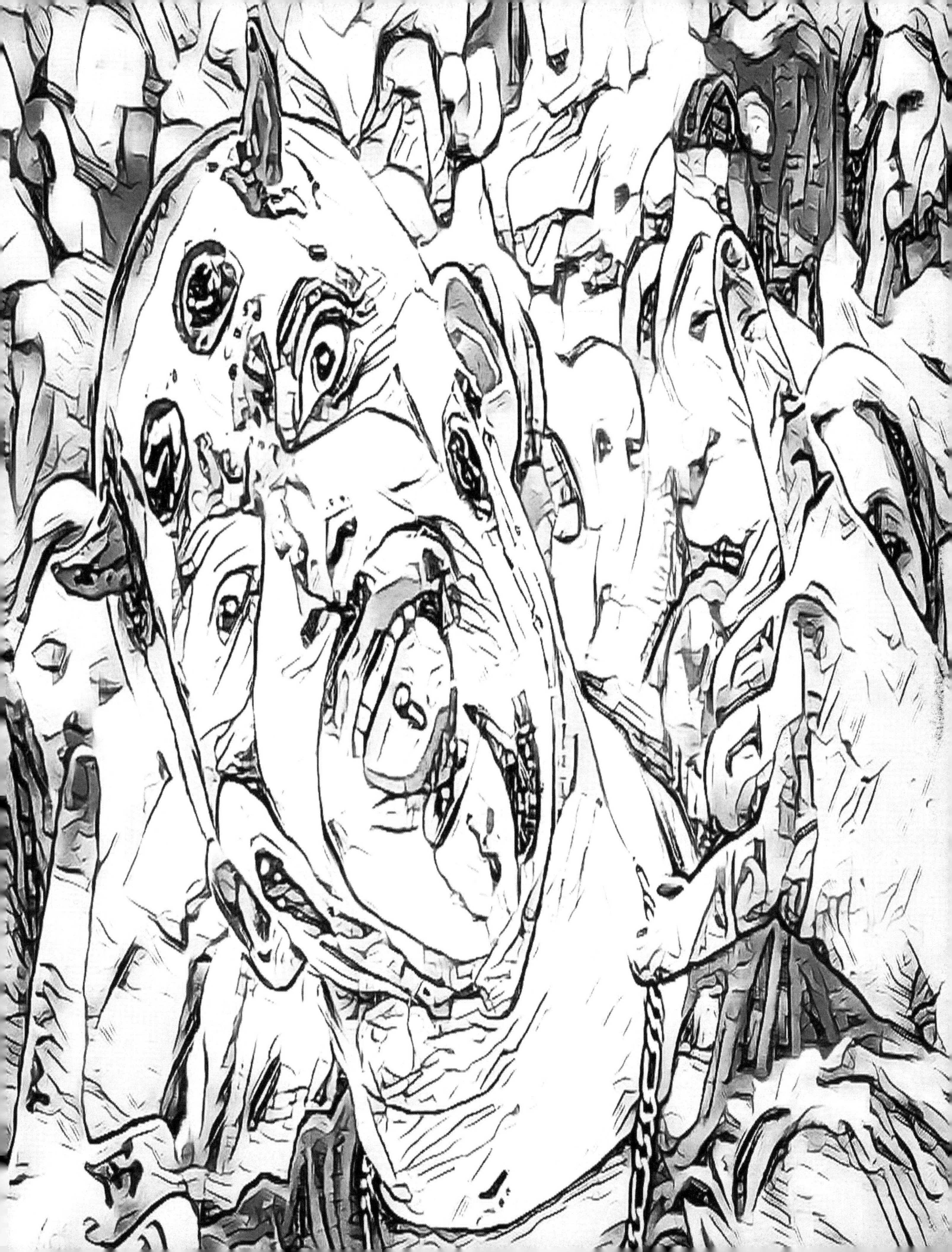

INSANE CLOWN POSSE

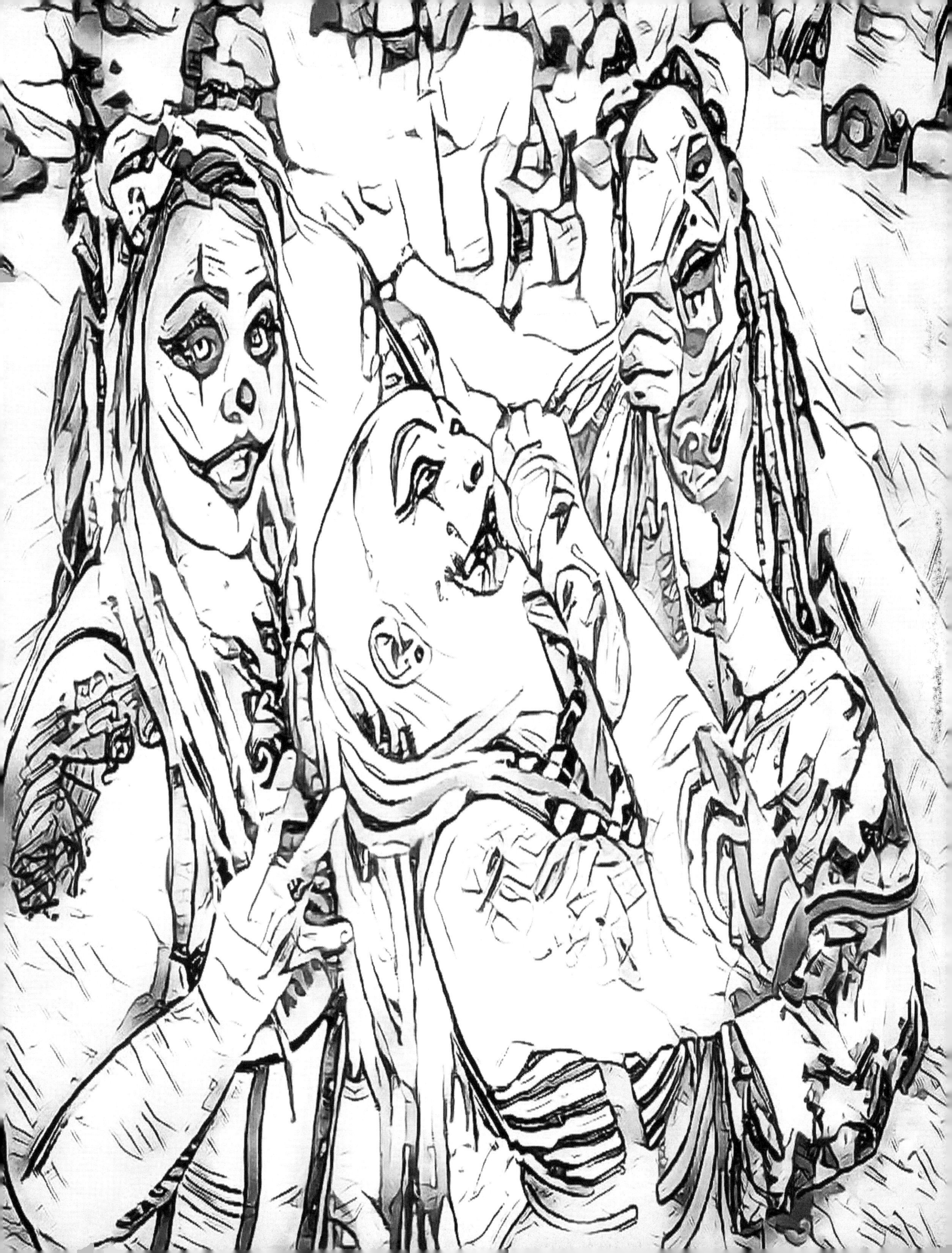

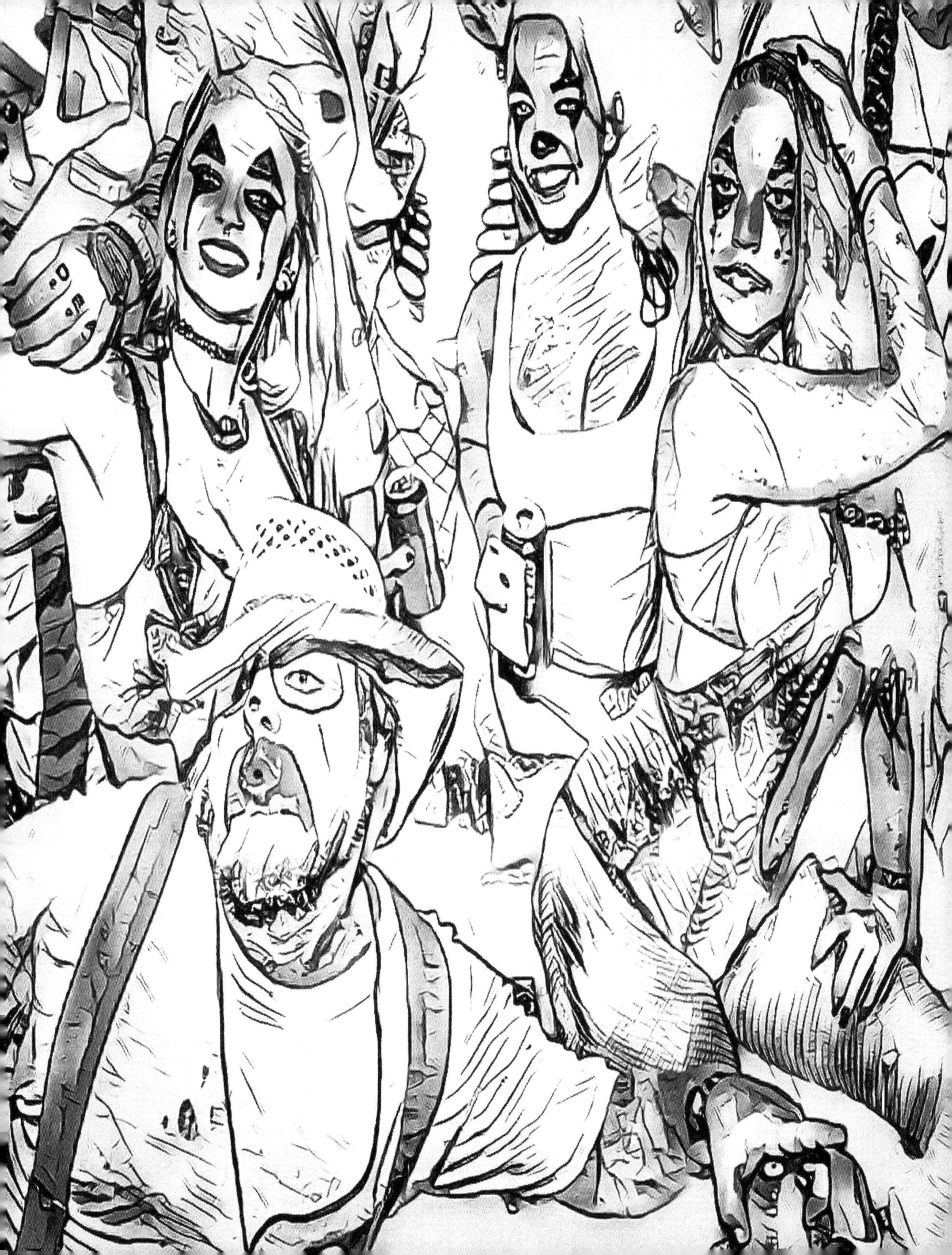

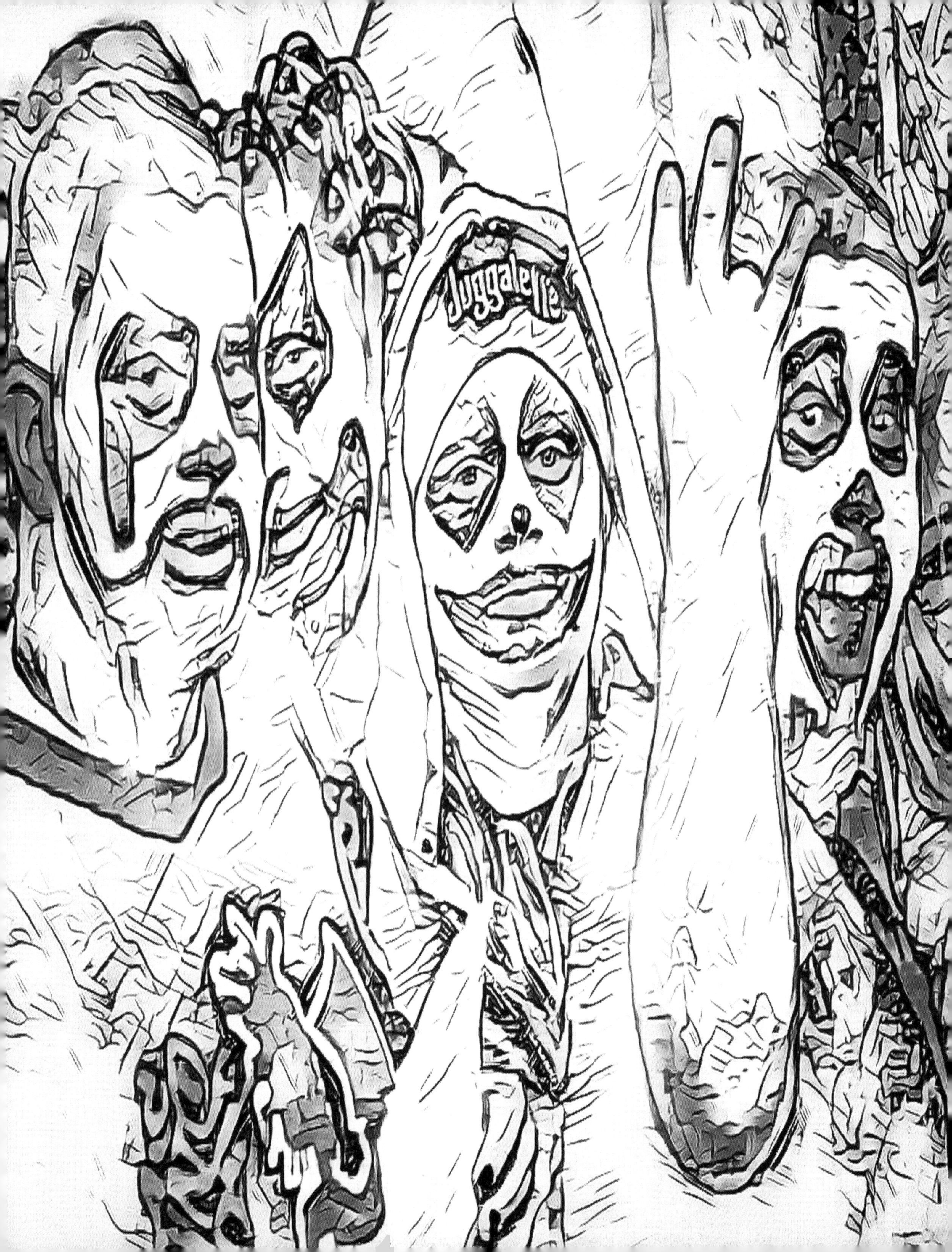
Juggalette

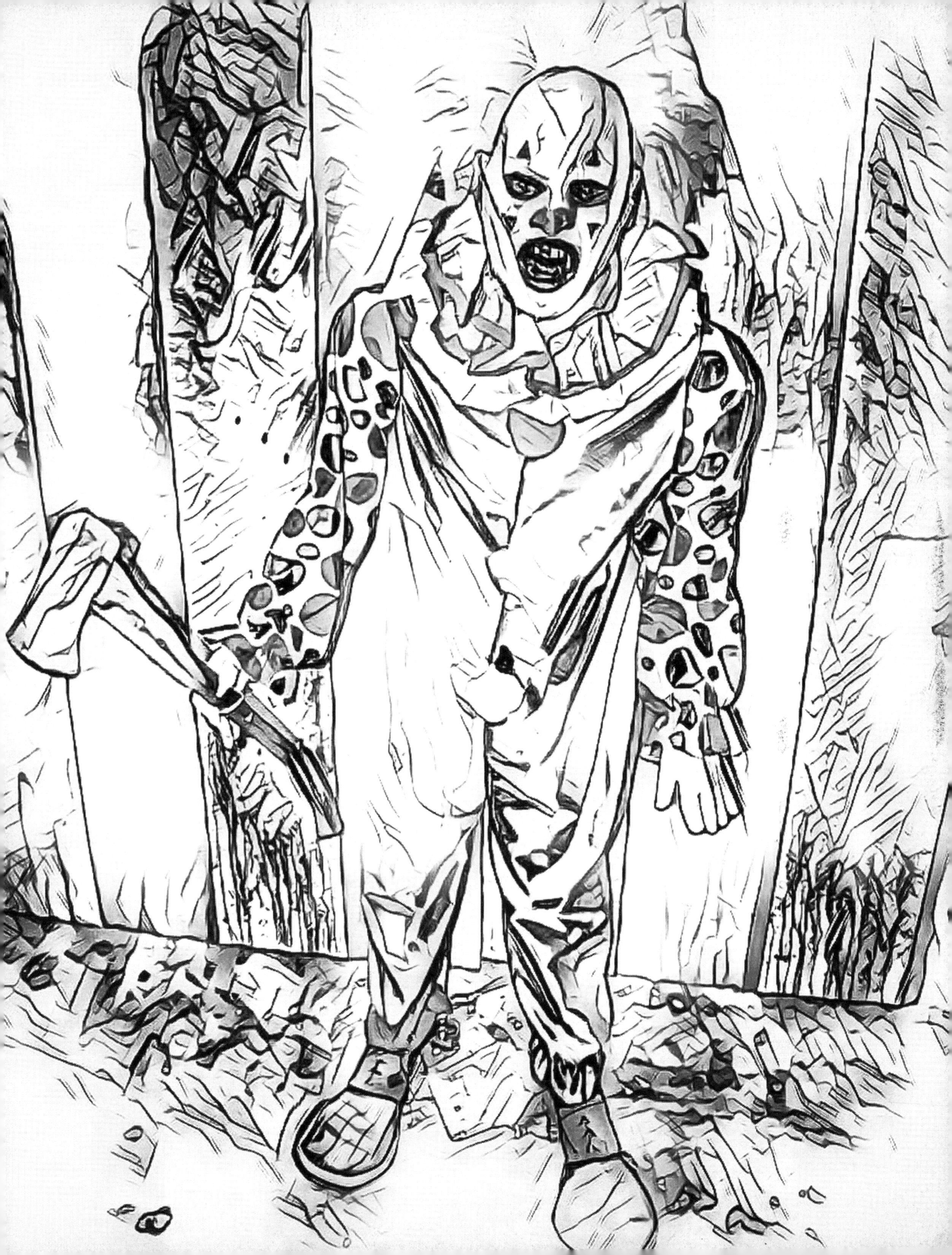

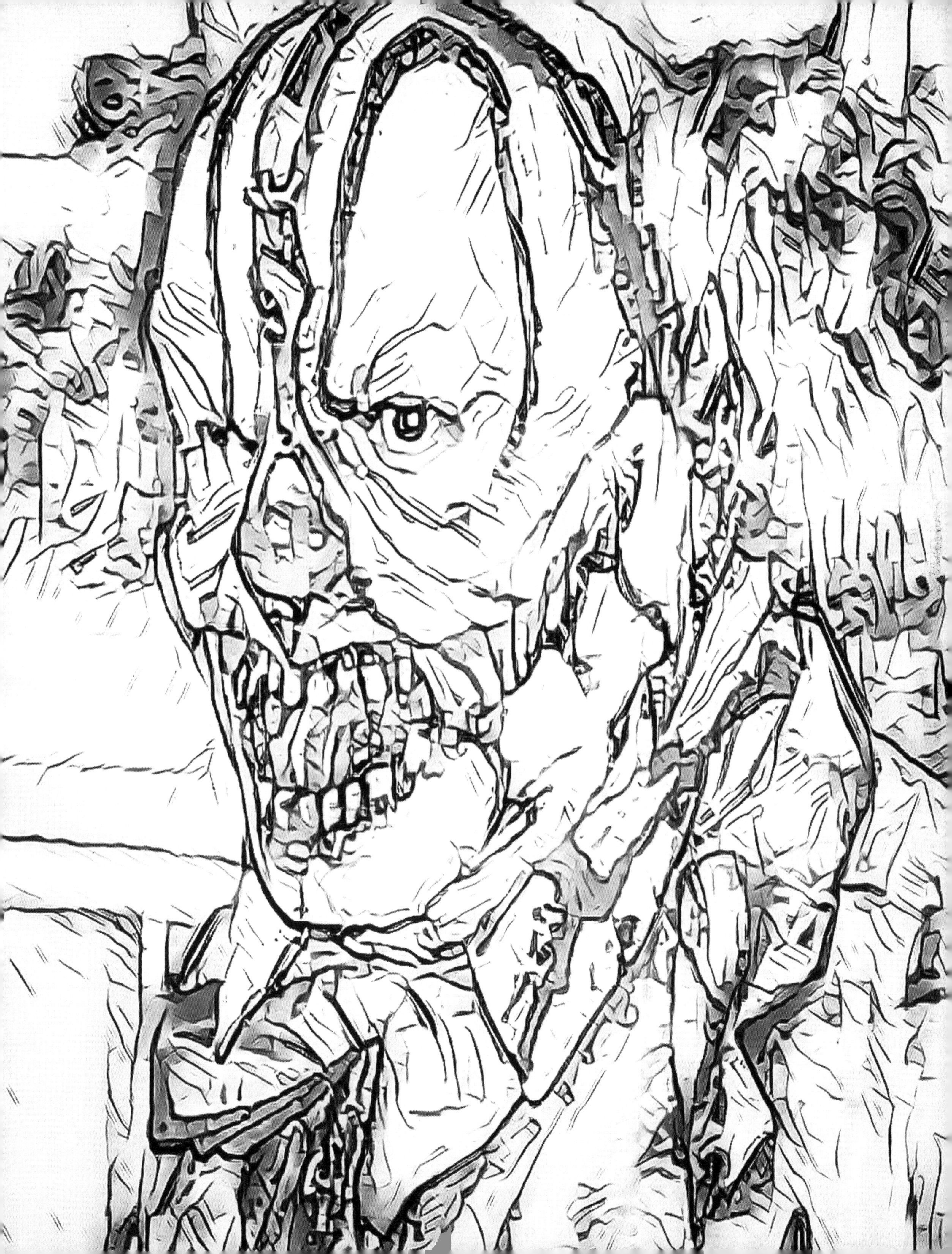

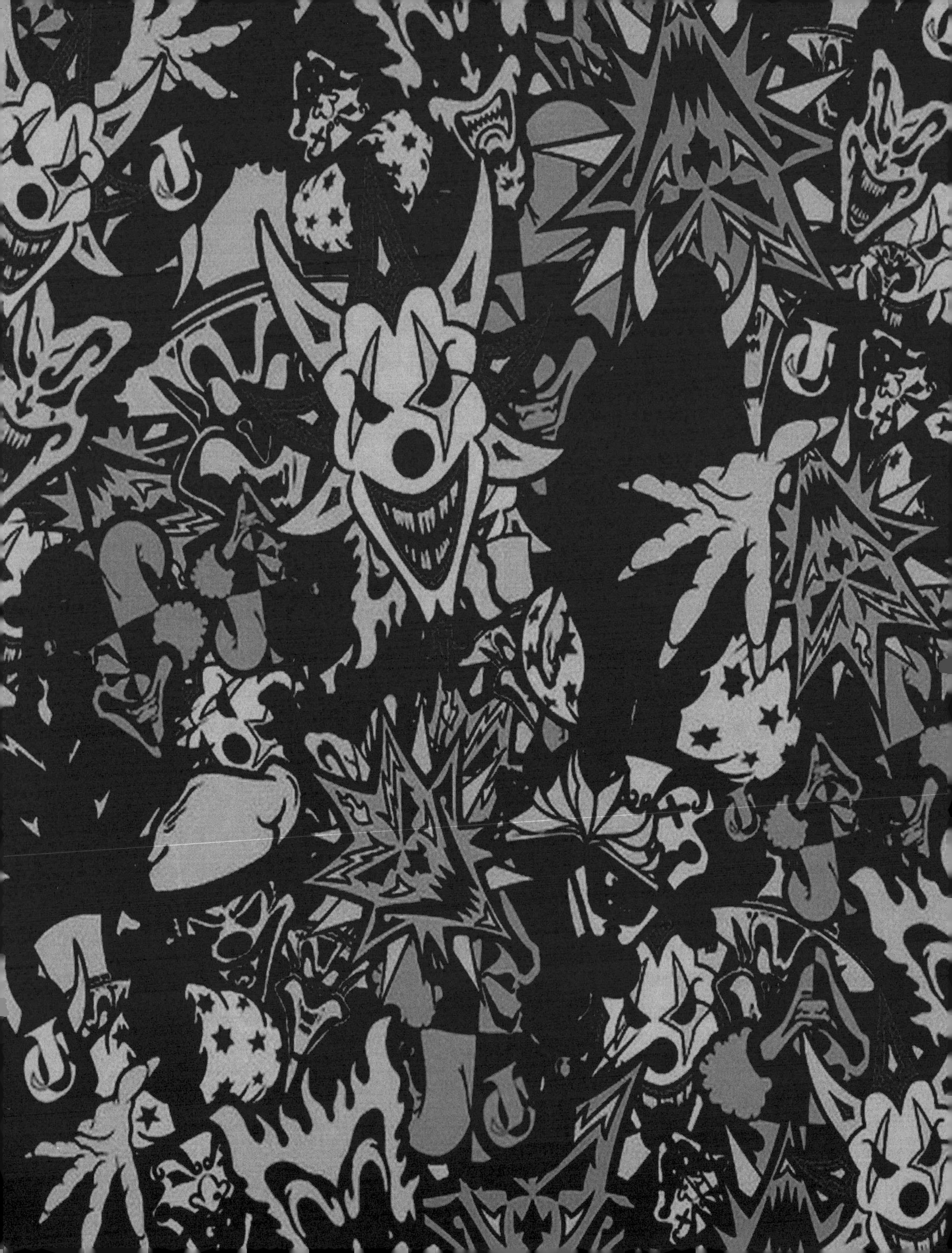

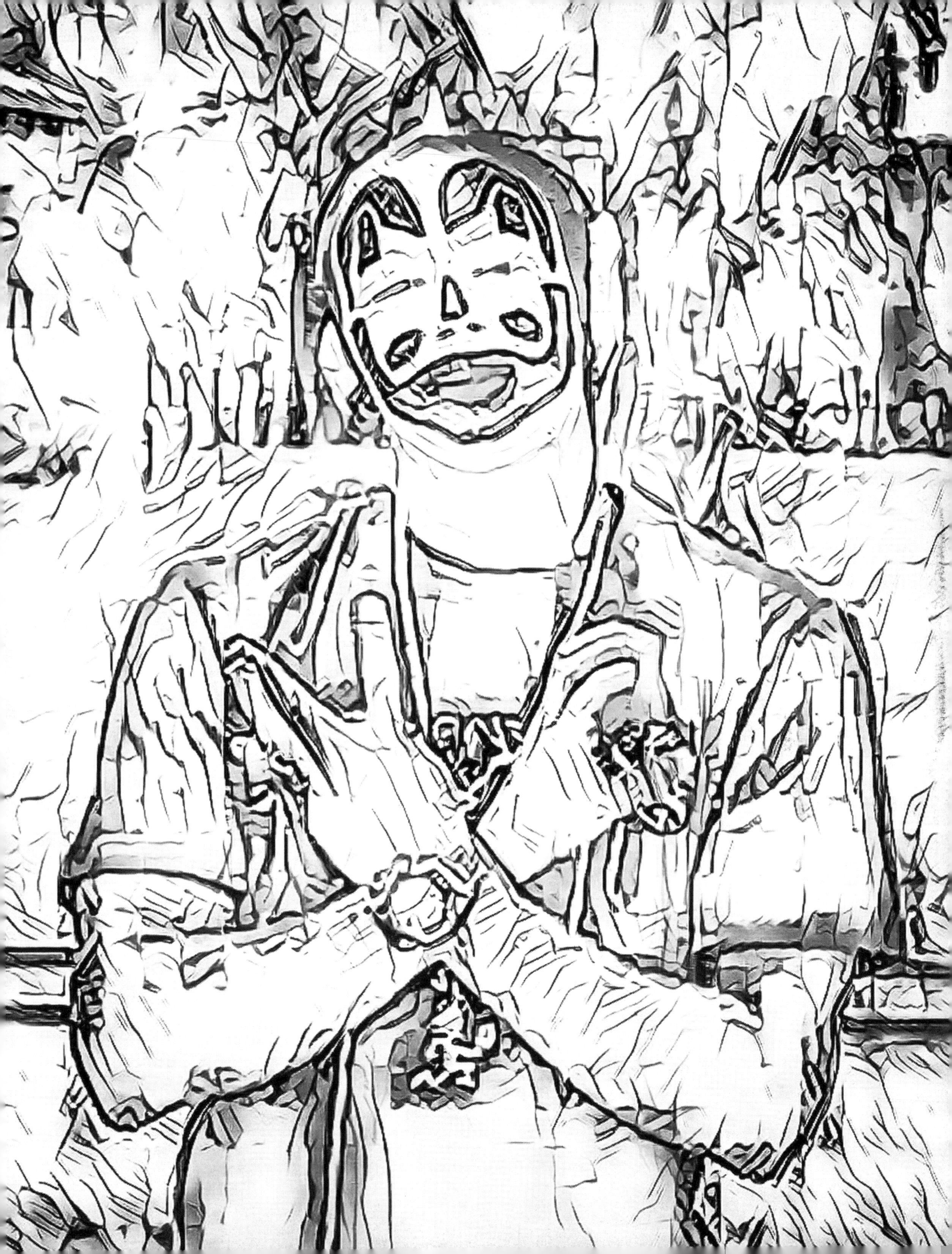

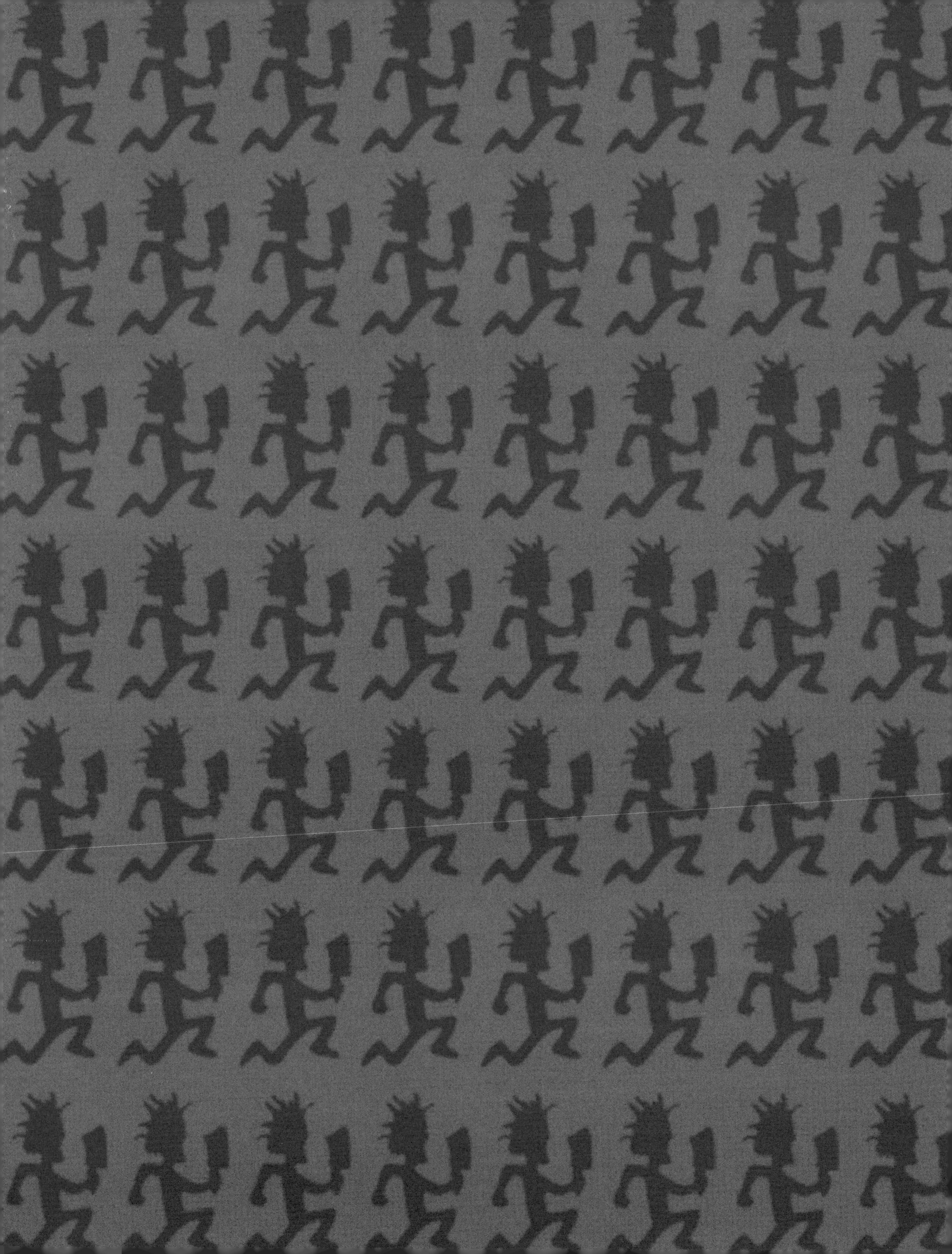

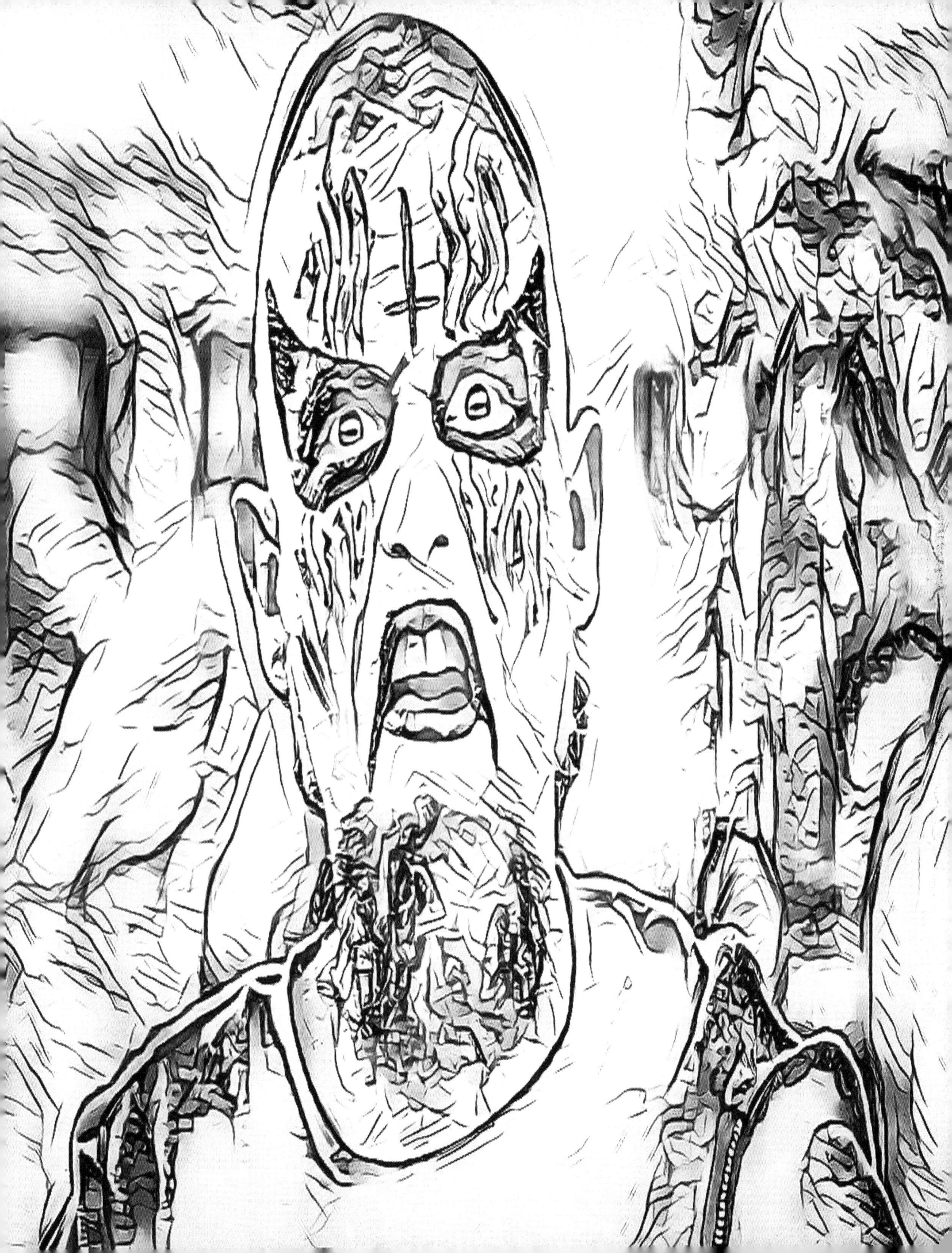

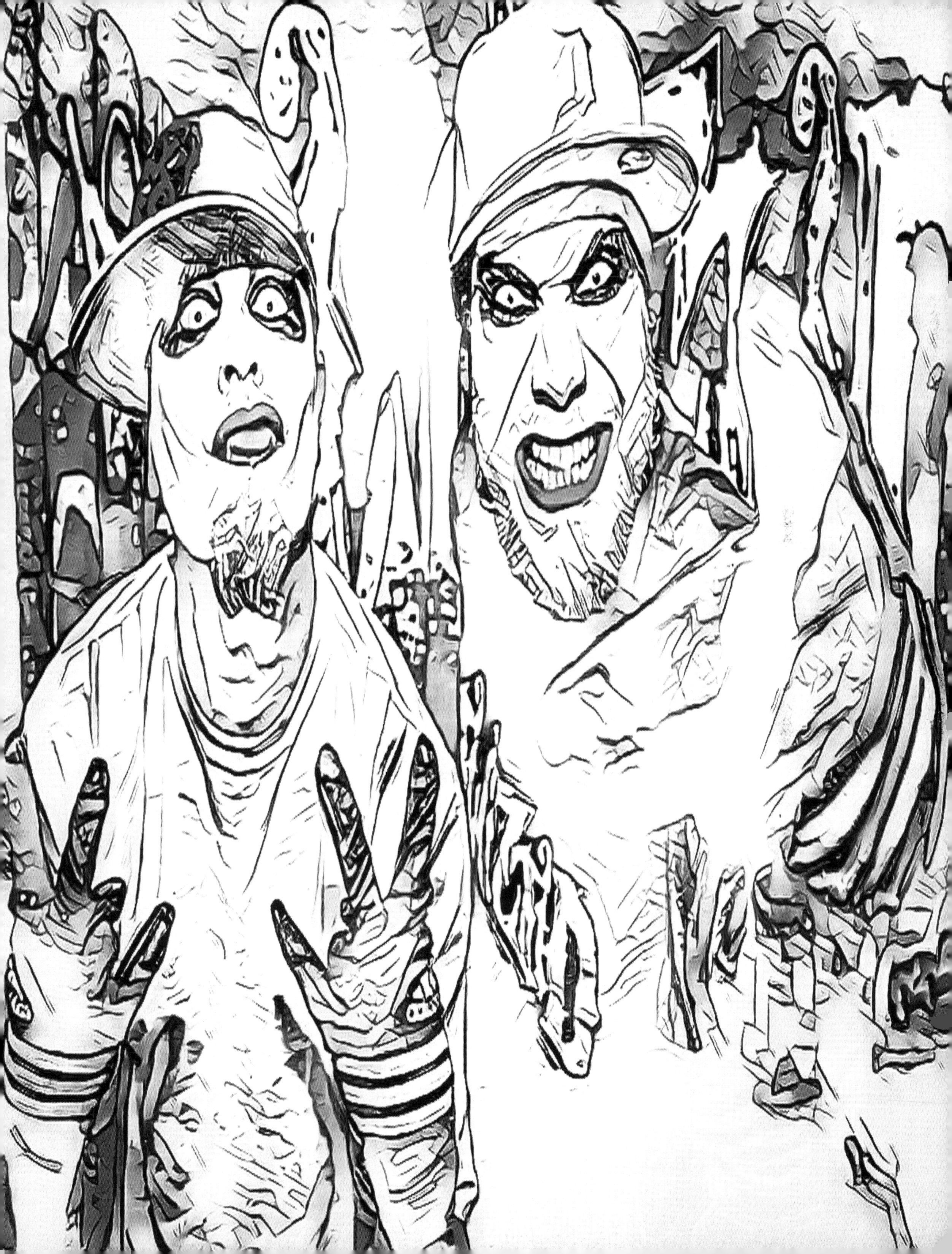

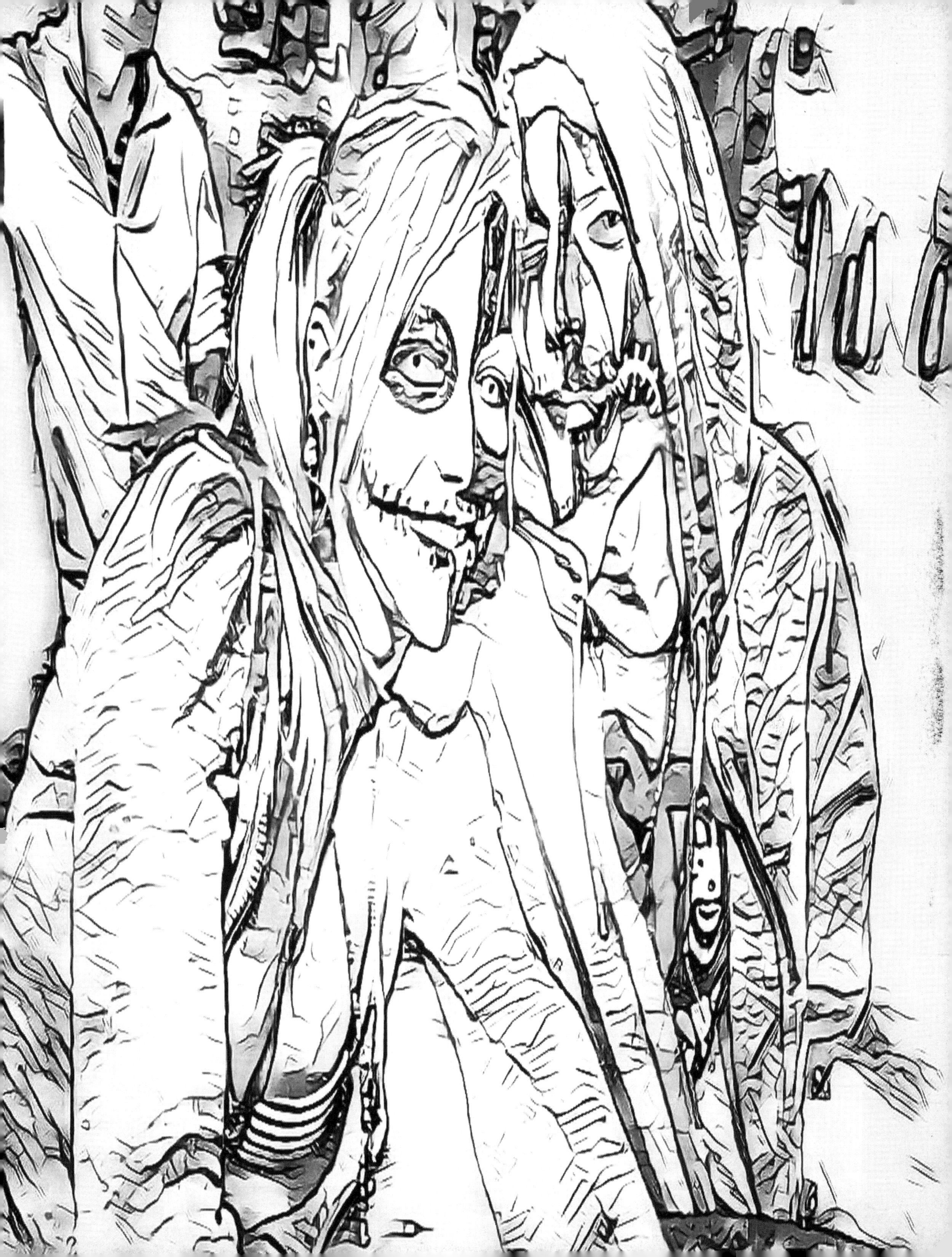

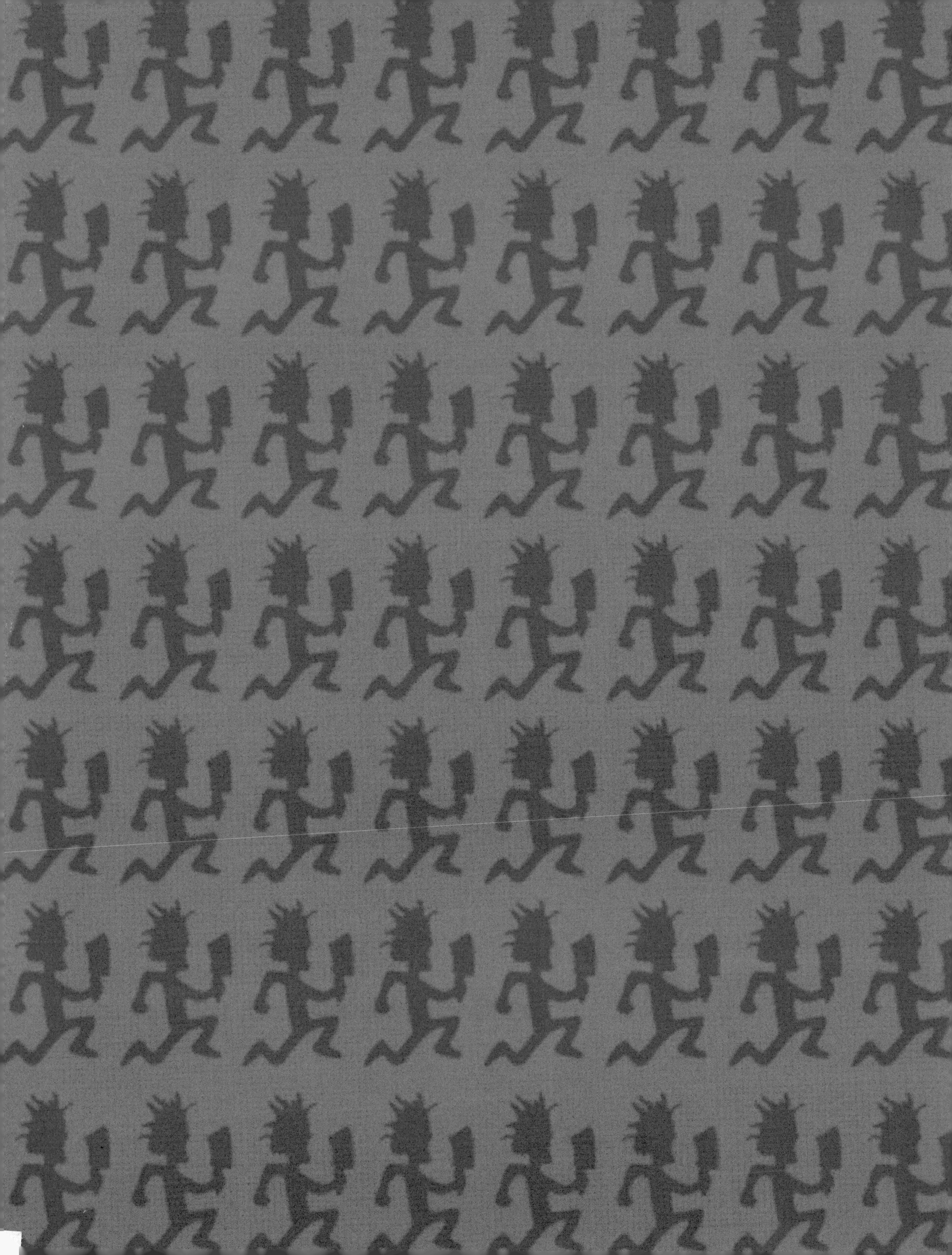

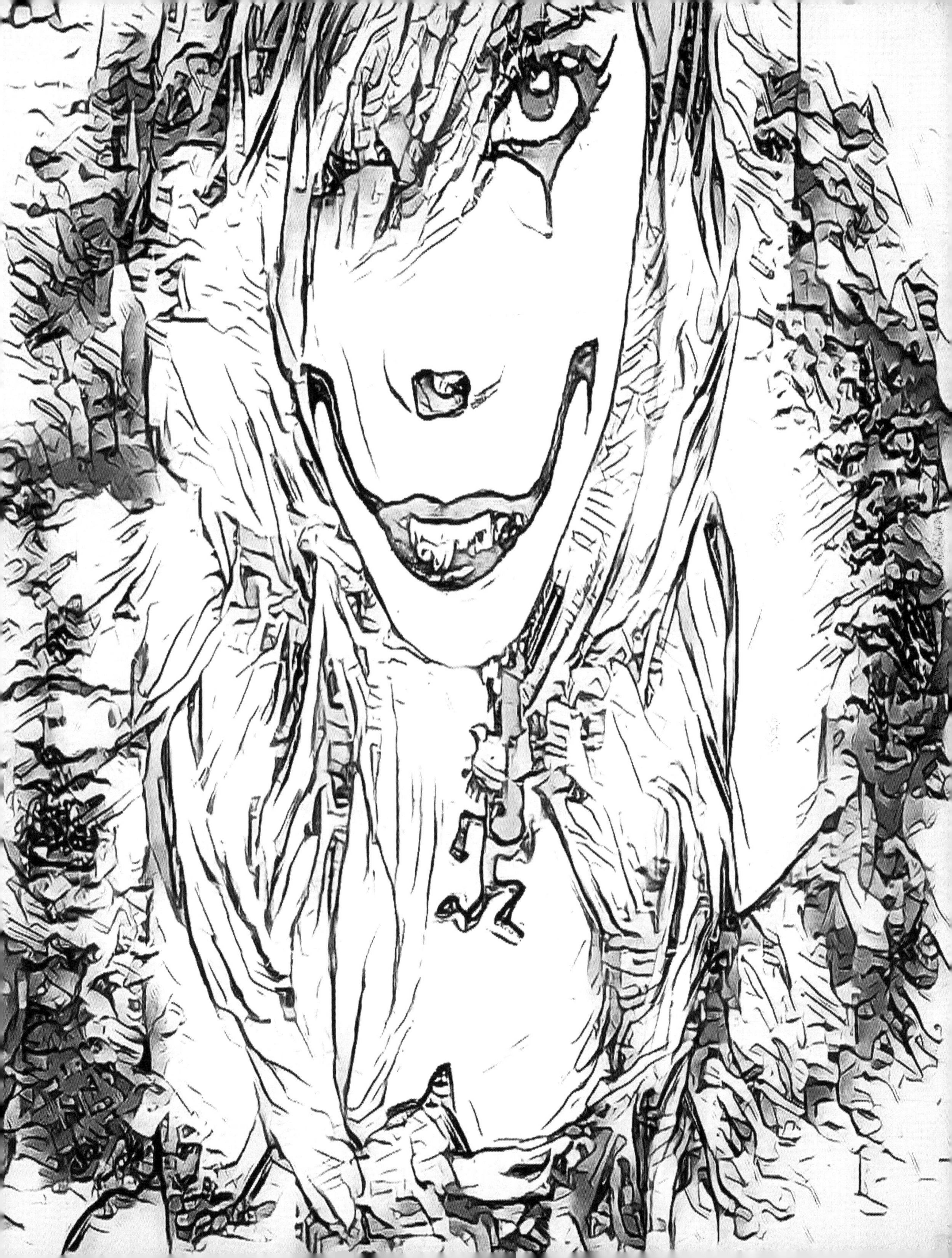

INSANE CLOWN POSSE

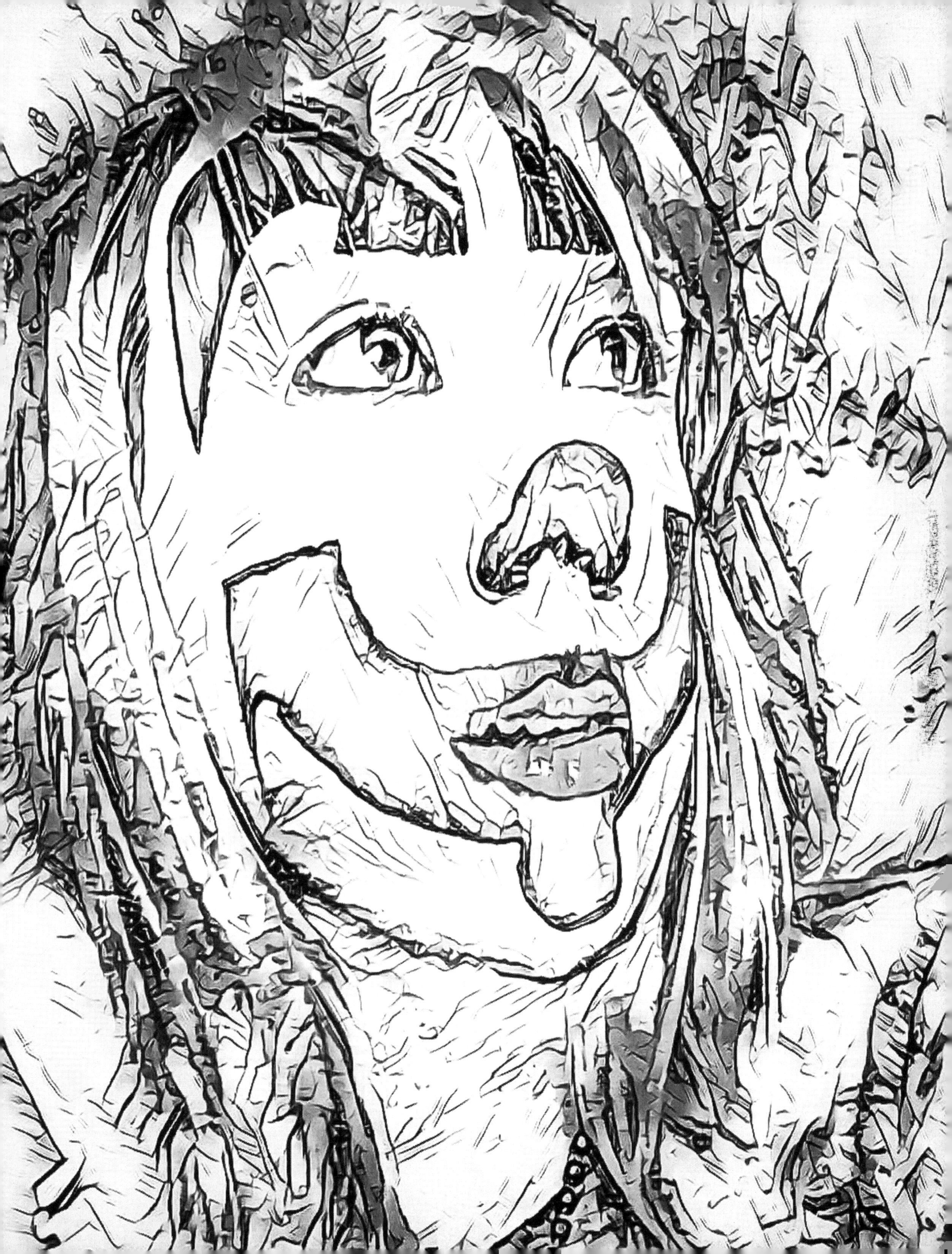

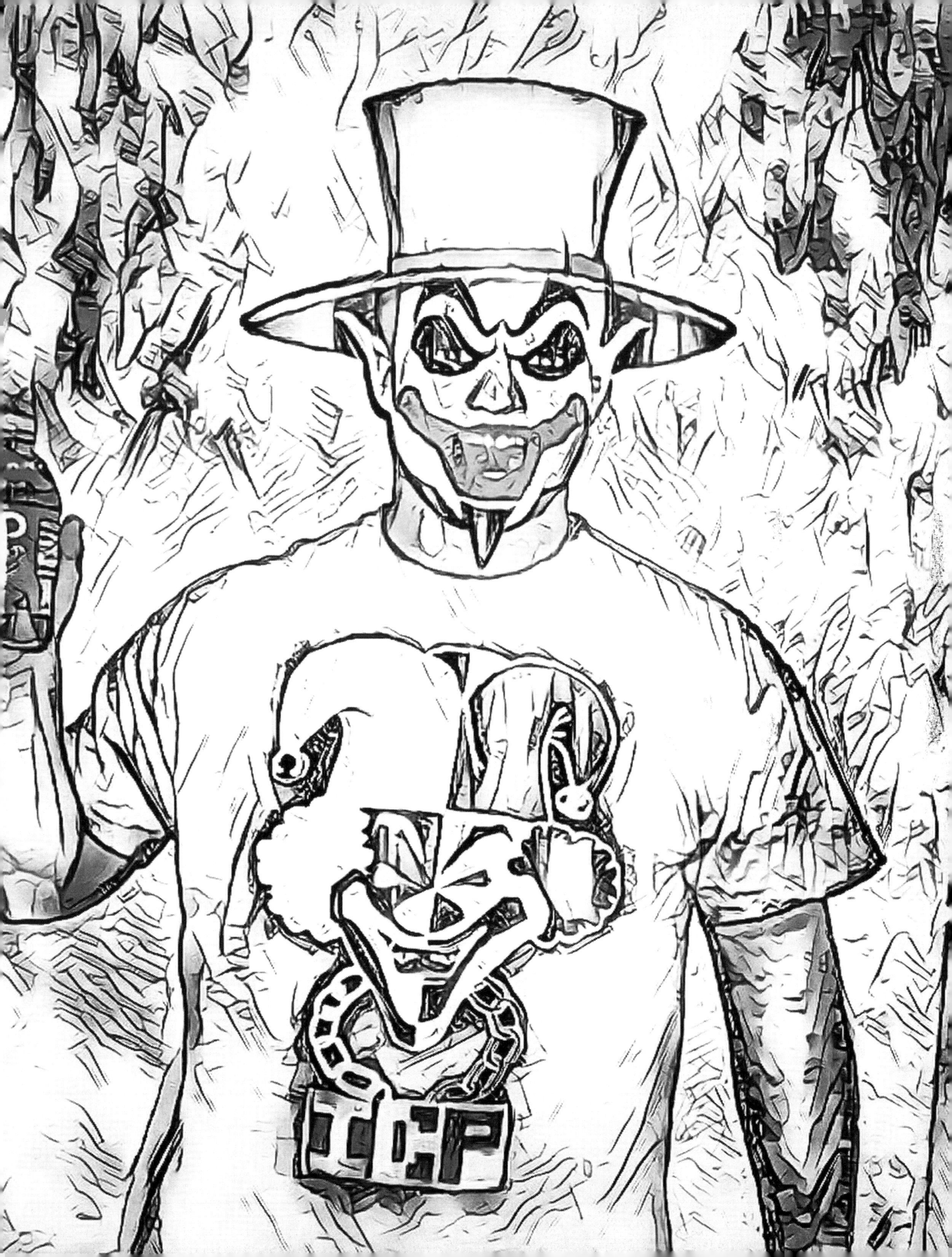
ICP

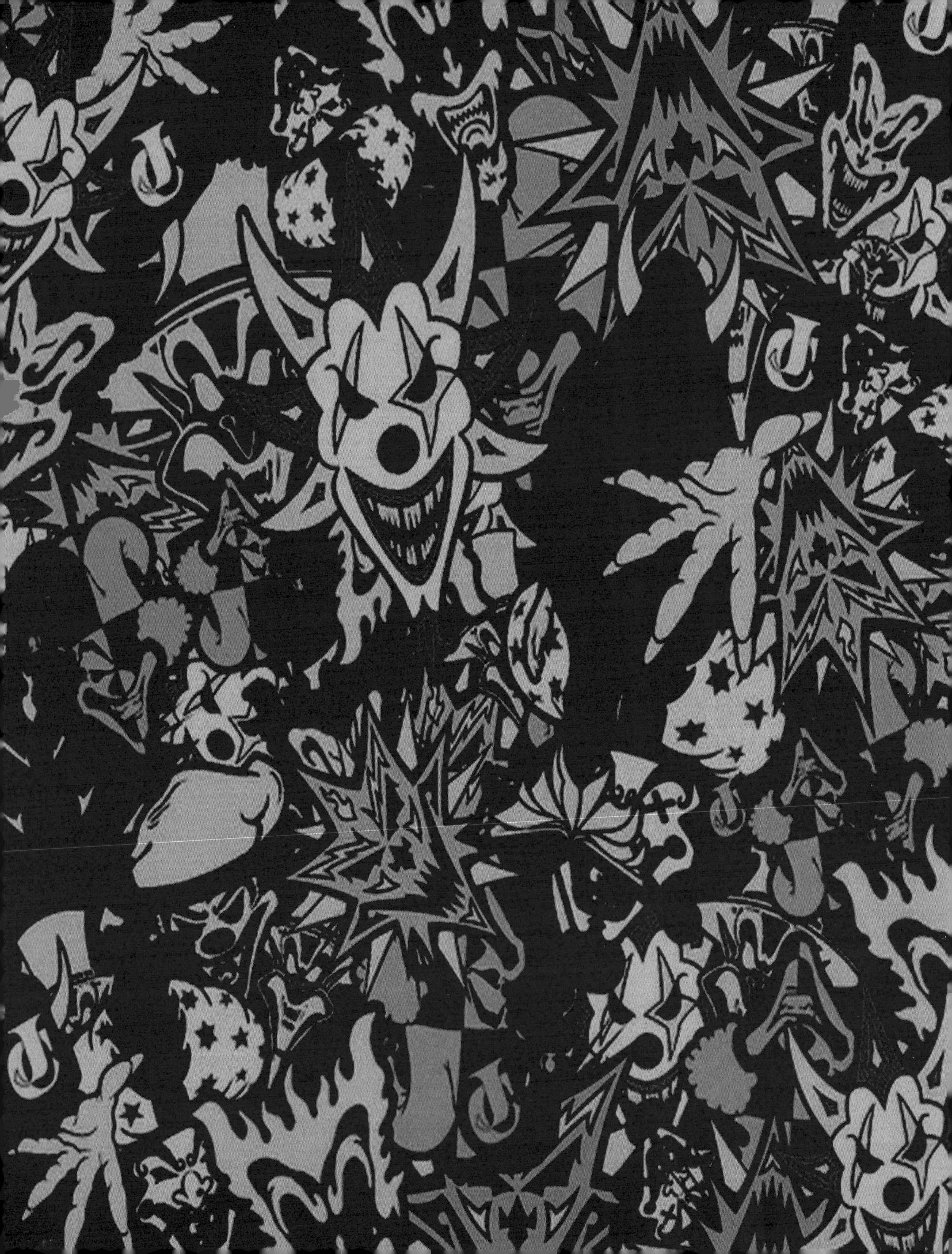

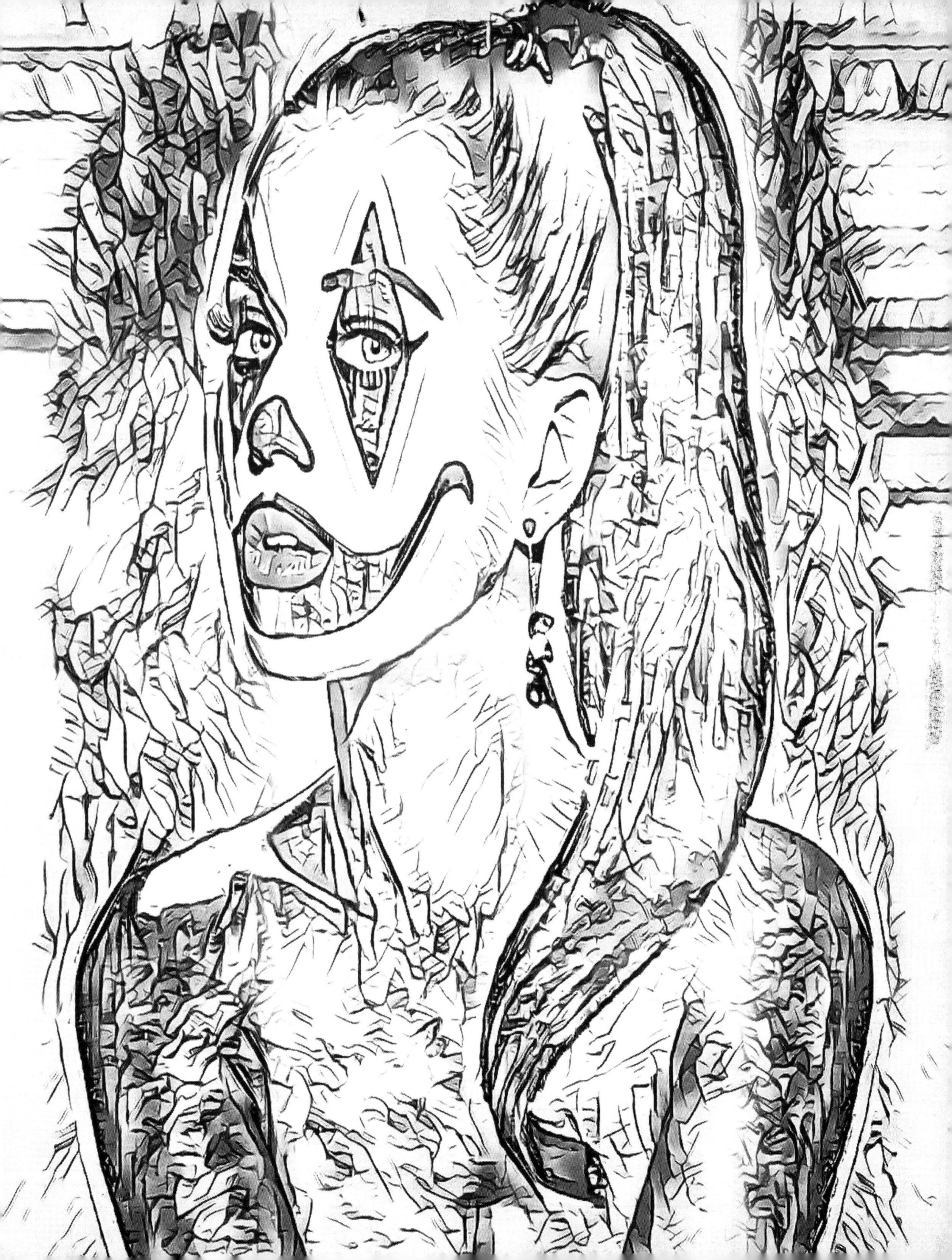

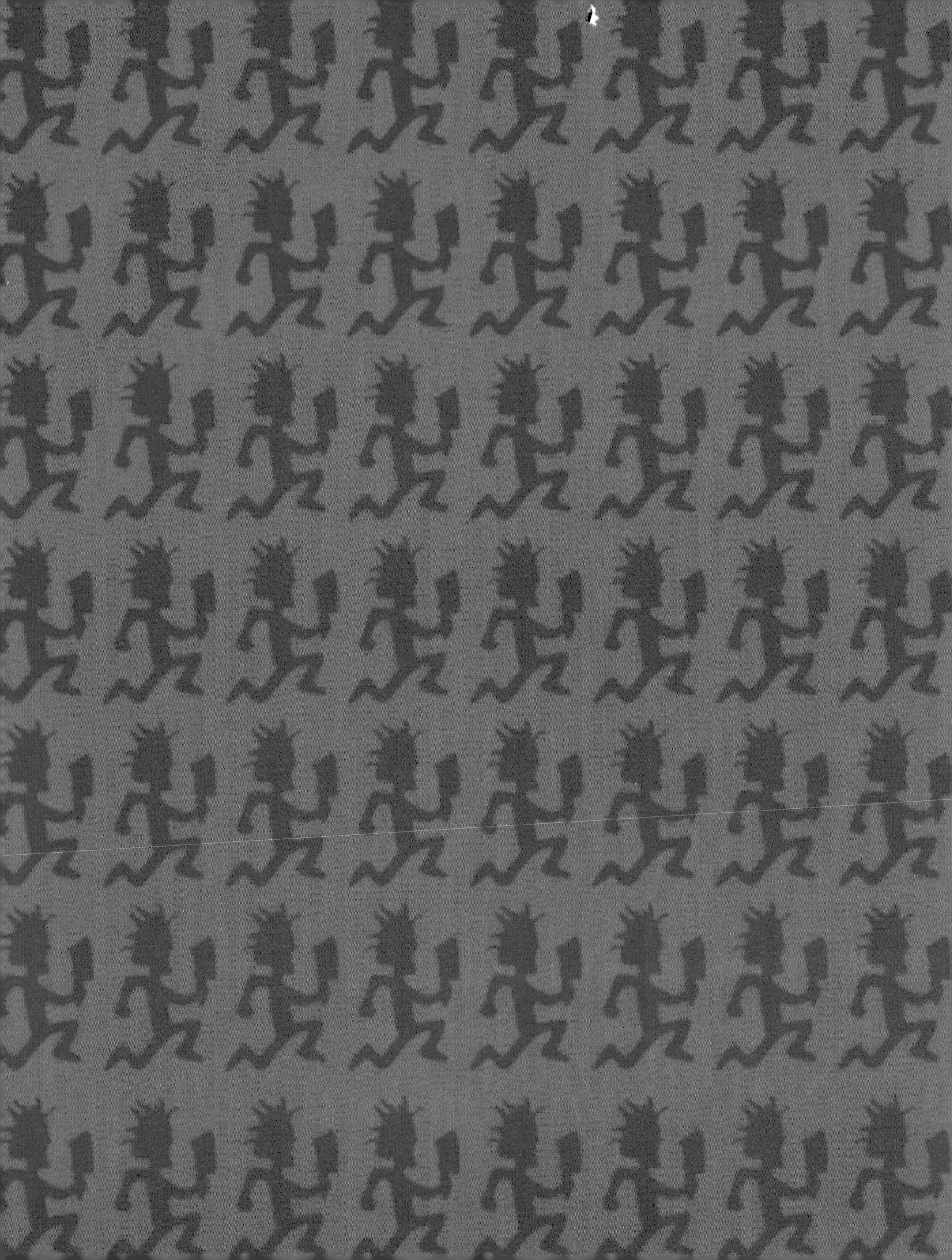

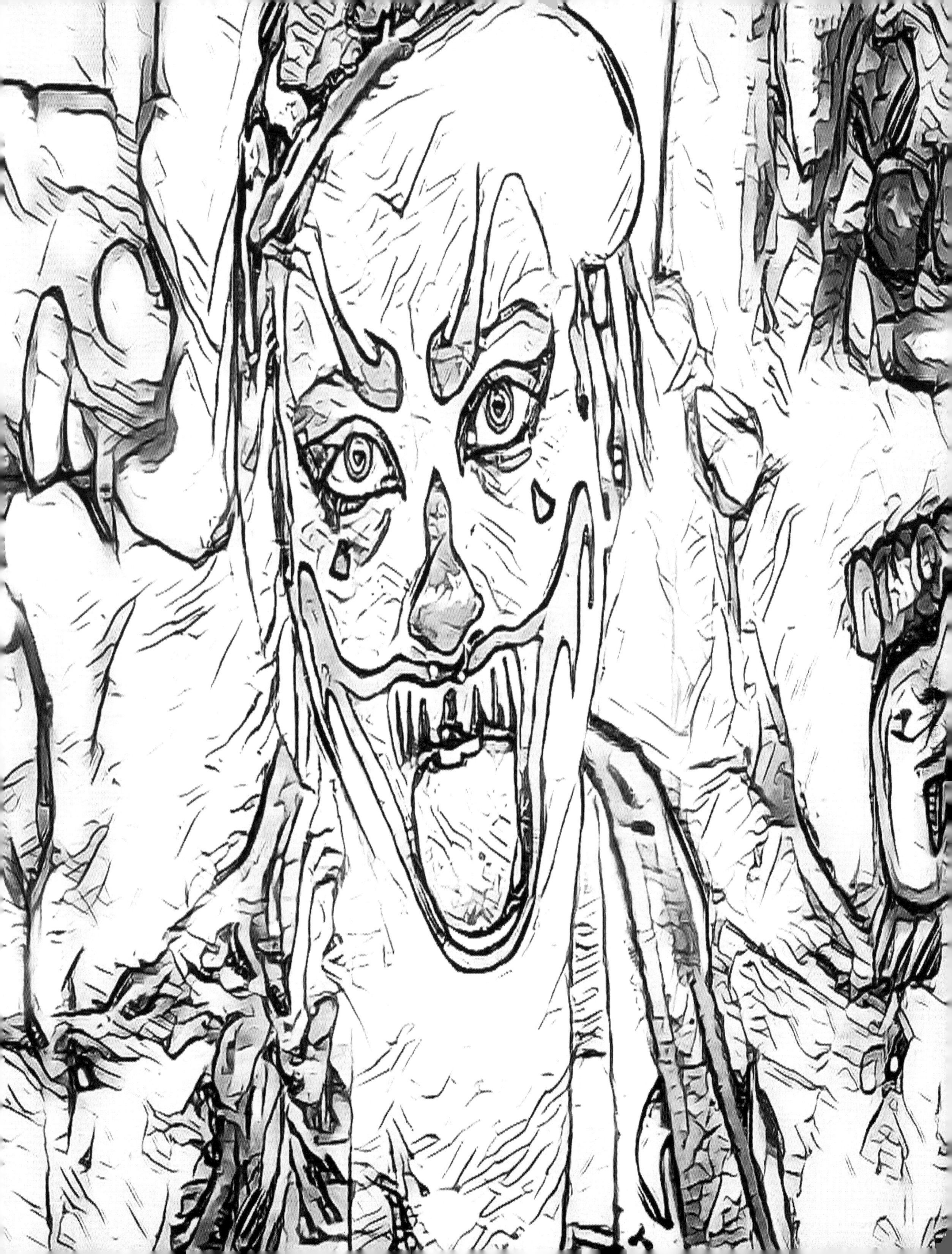

INSANE CLOWN POSSE

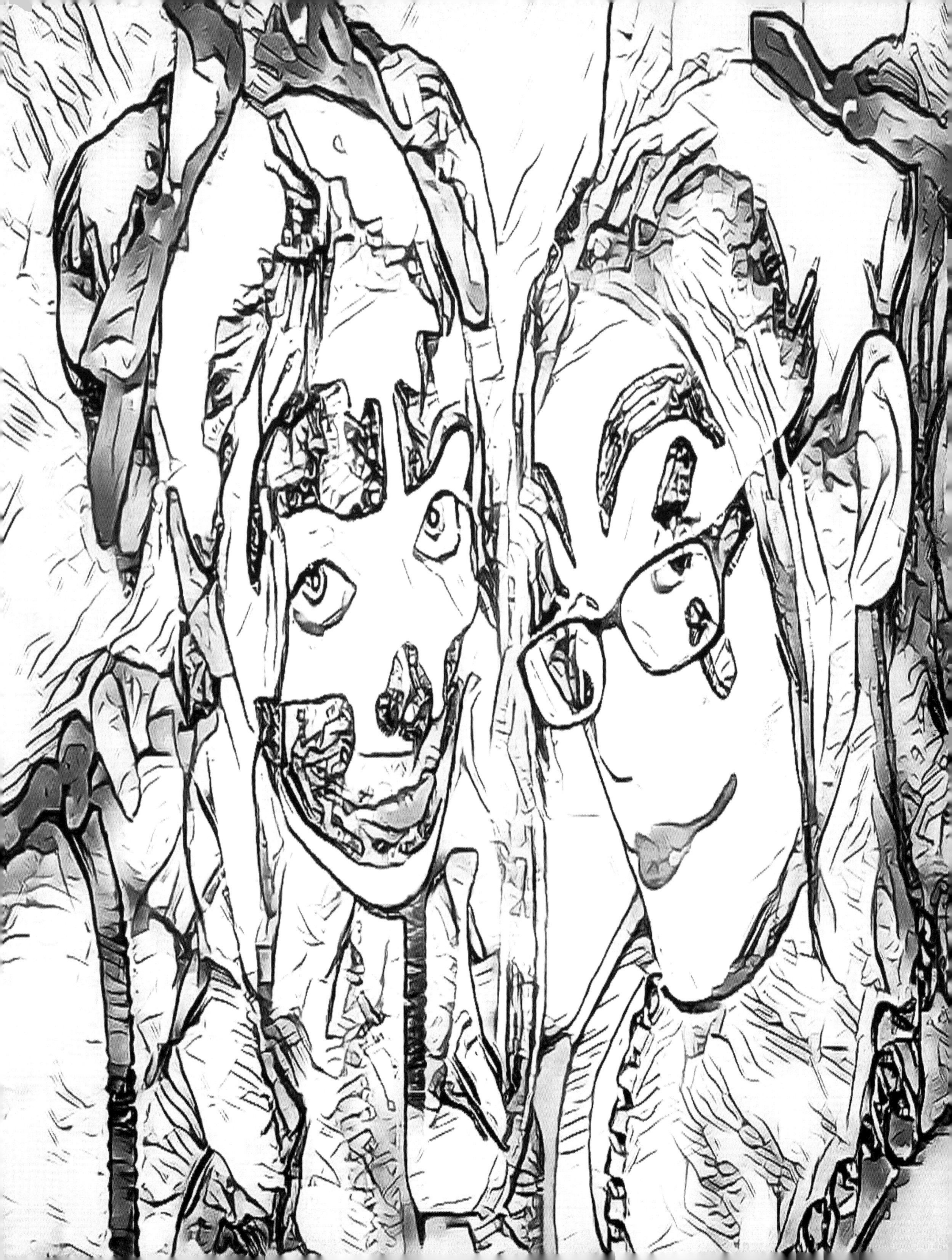

INSANE CLOWN POSSE

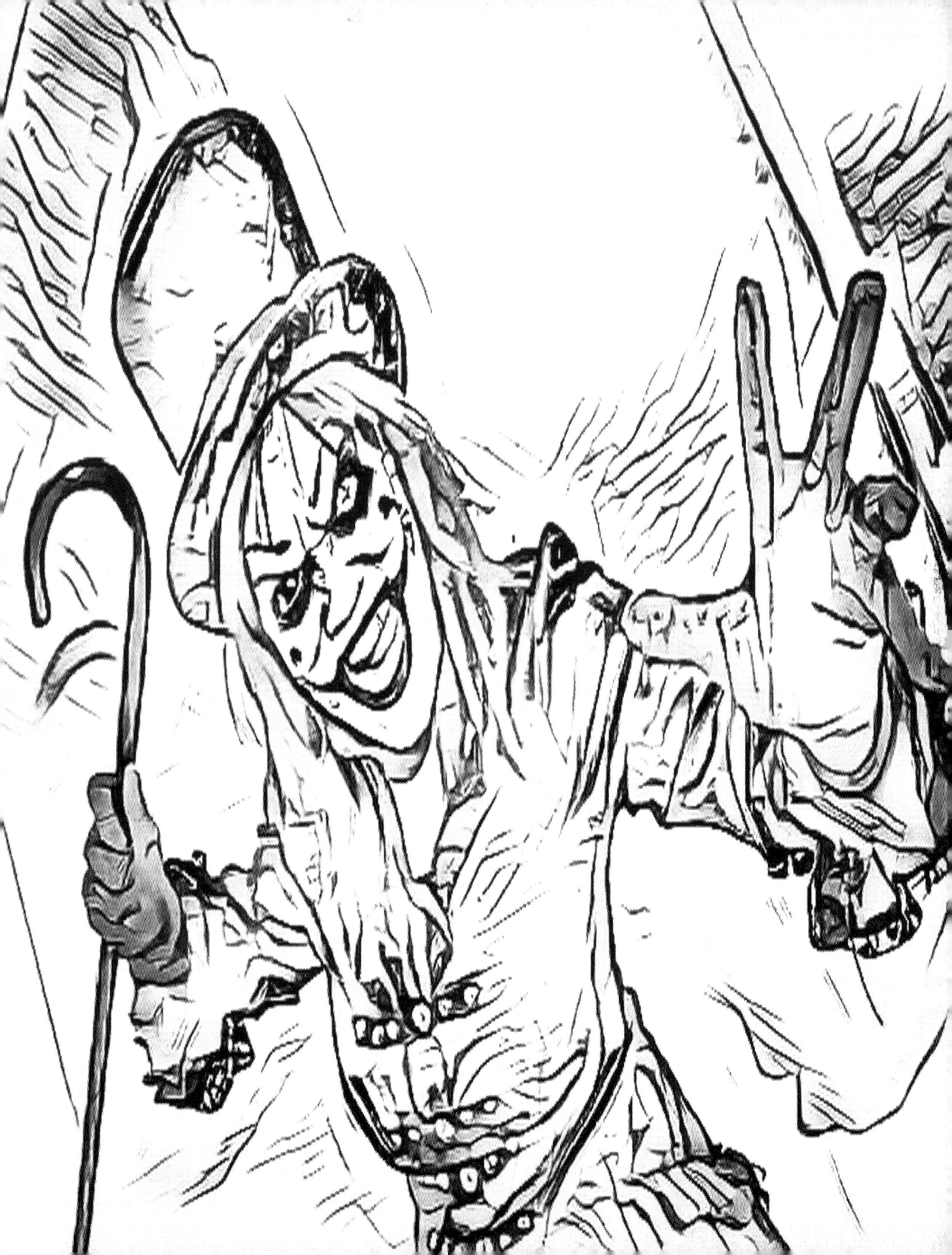

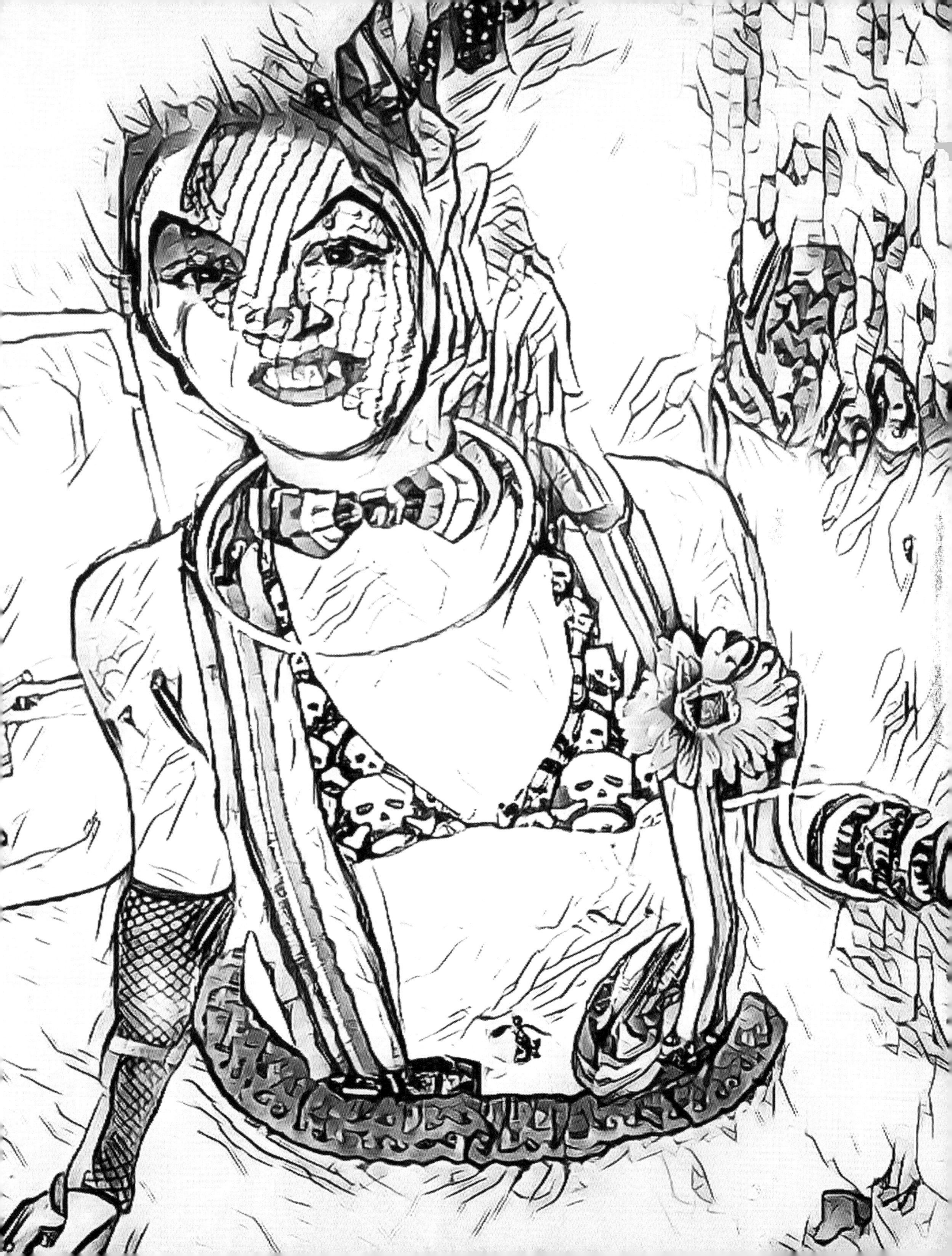

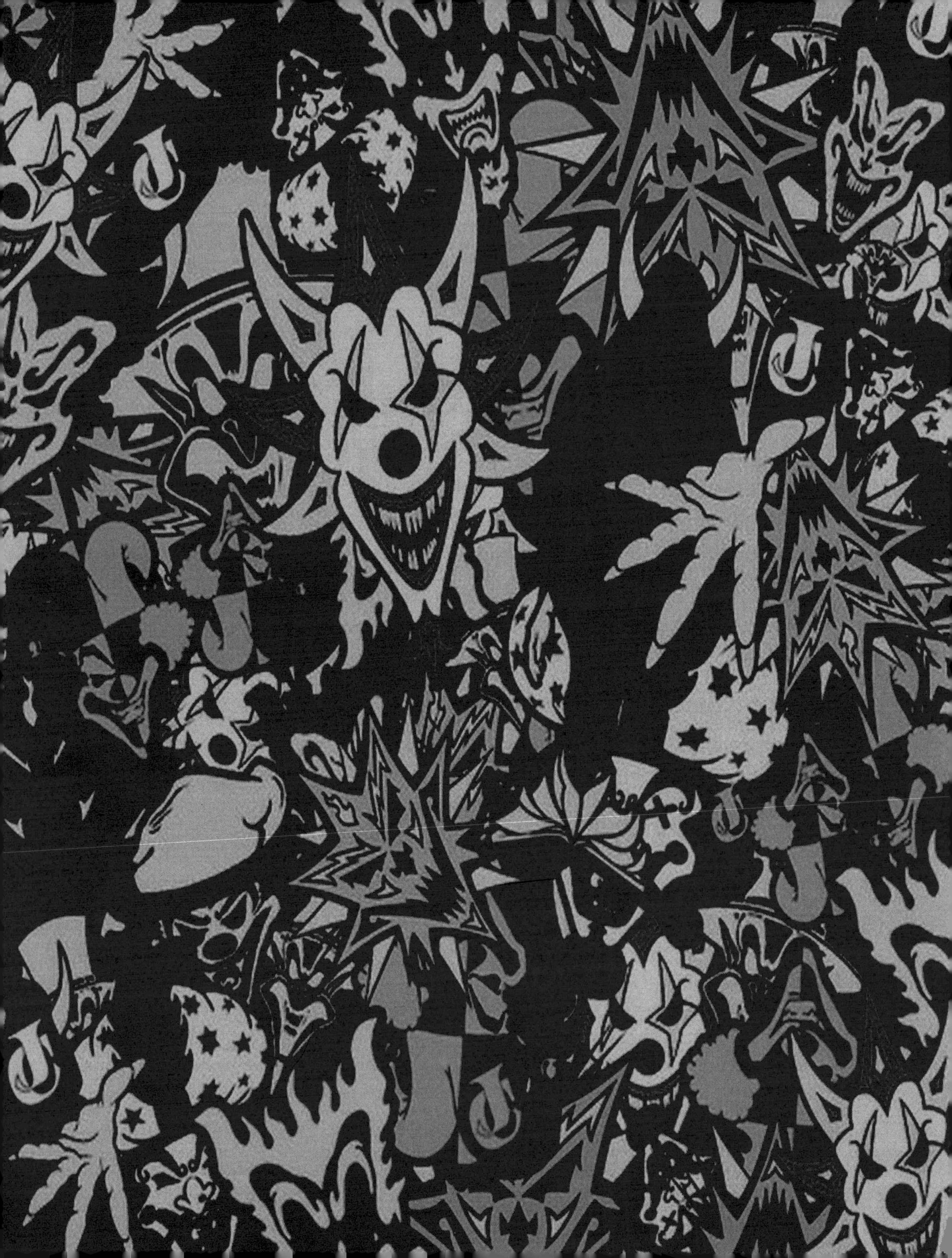

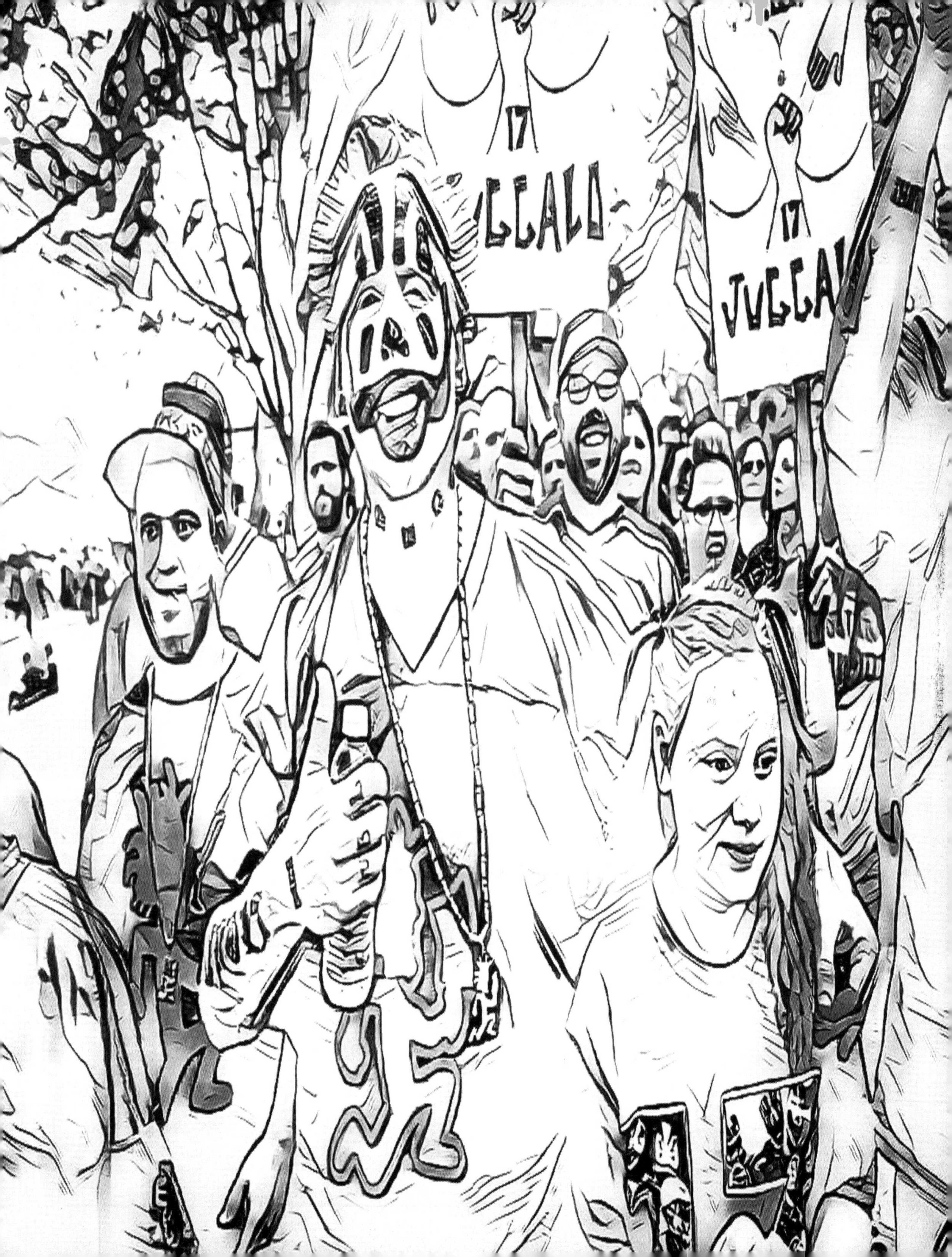
17
CCALO
17
JUGGA
17
JUGGAI

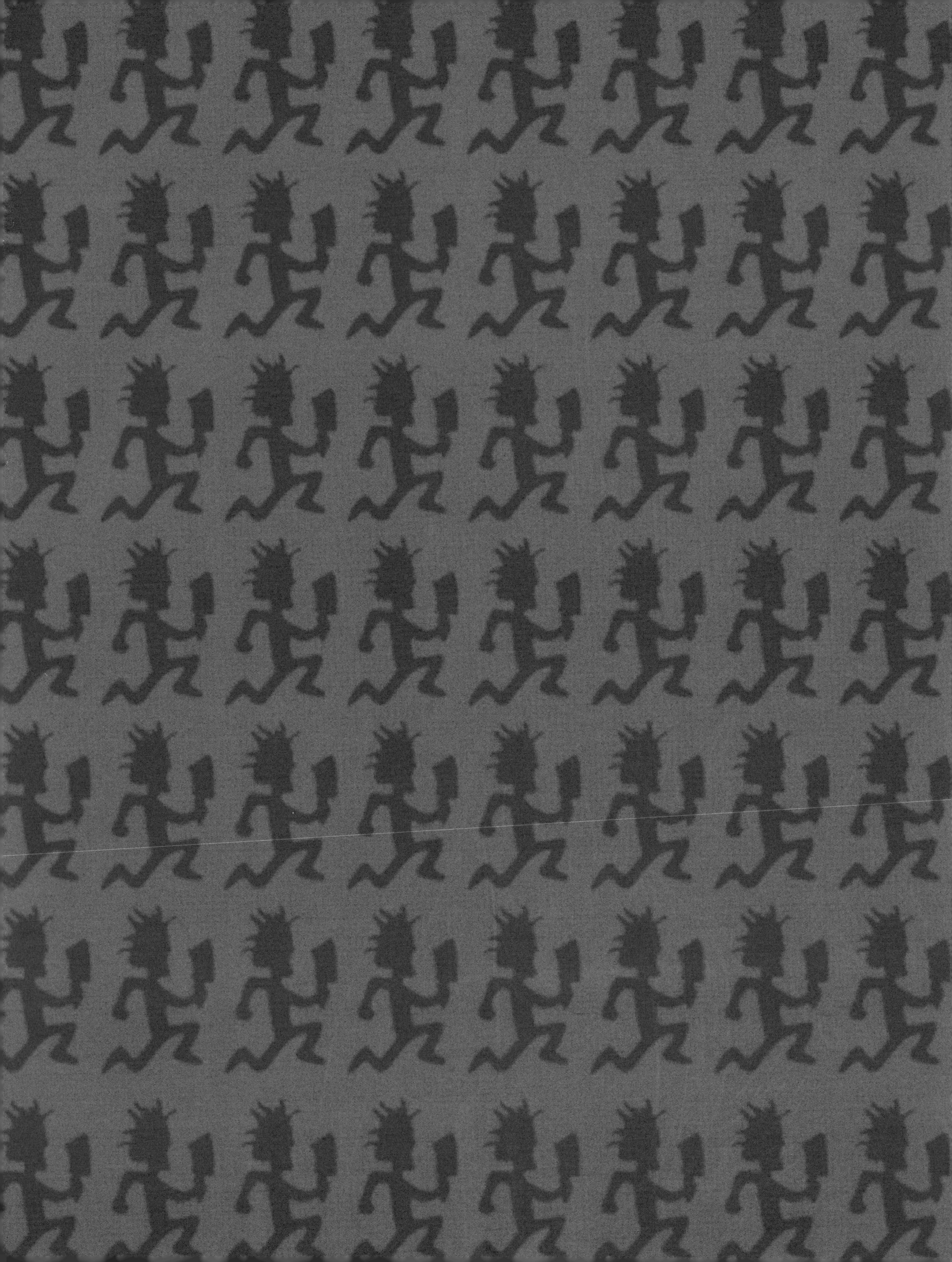

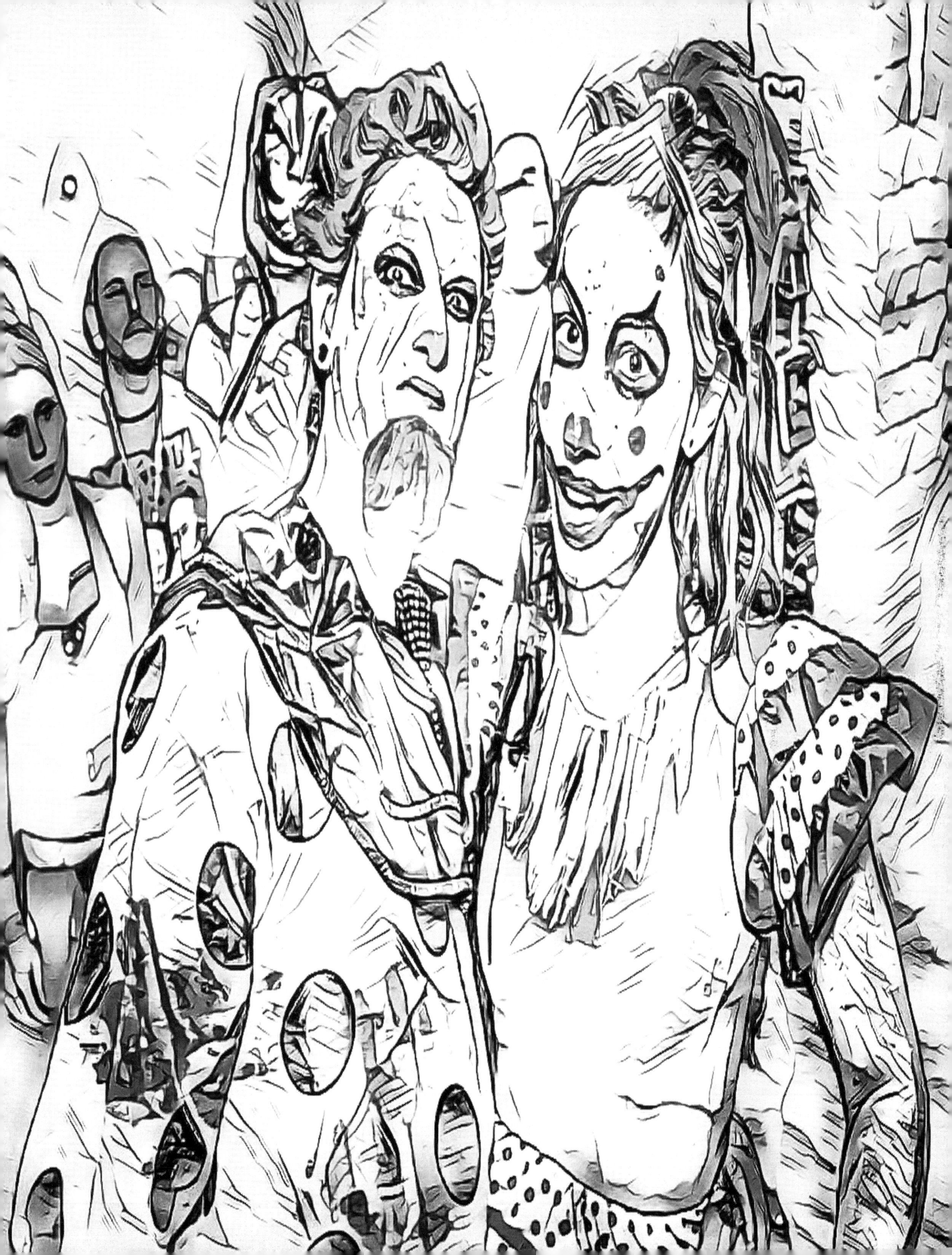

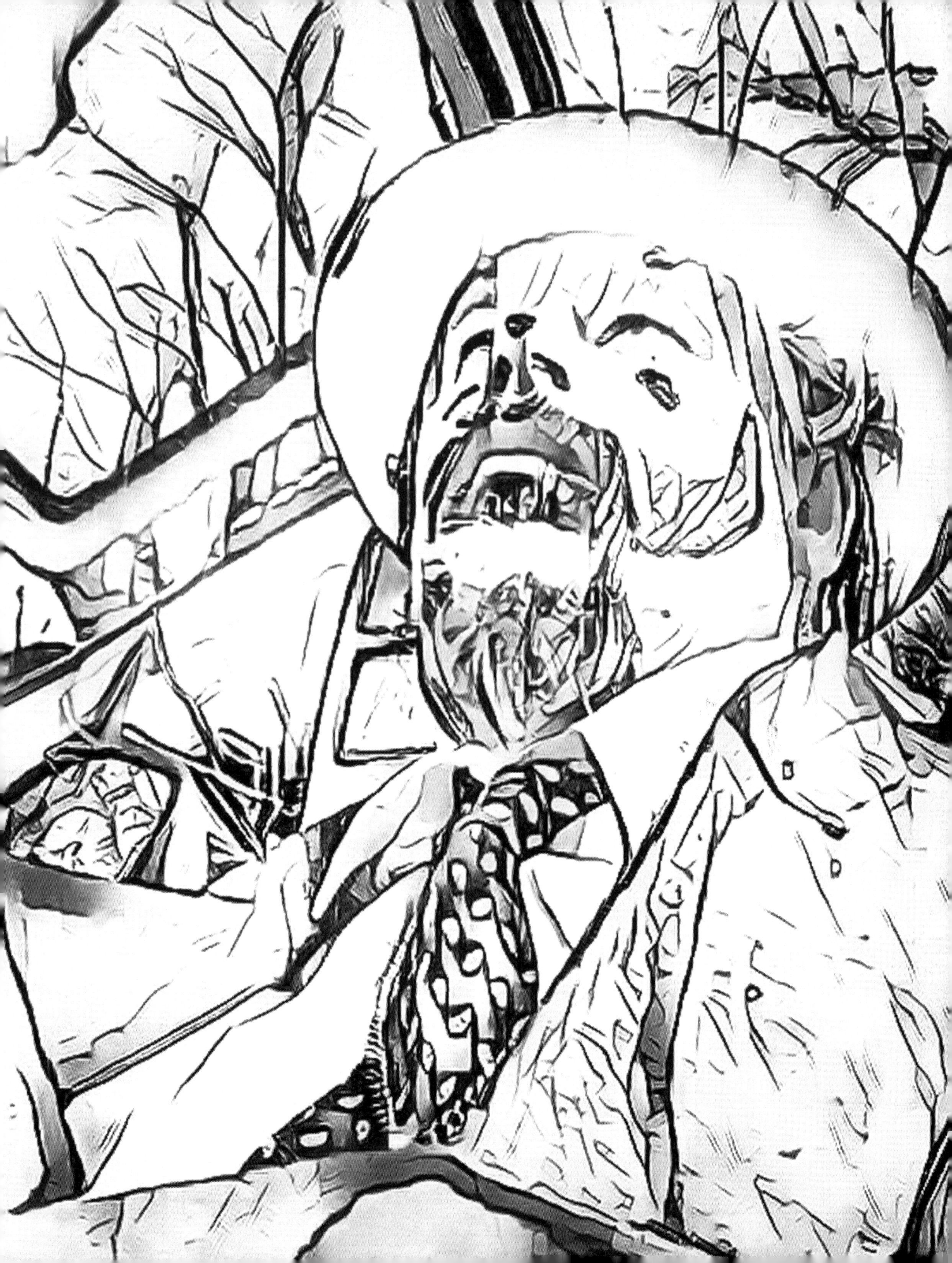

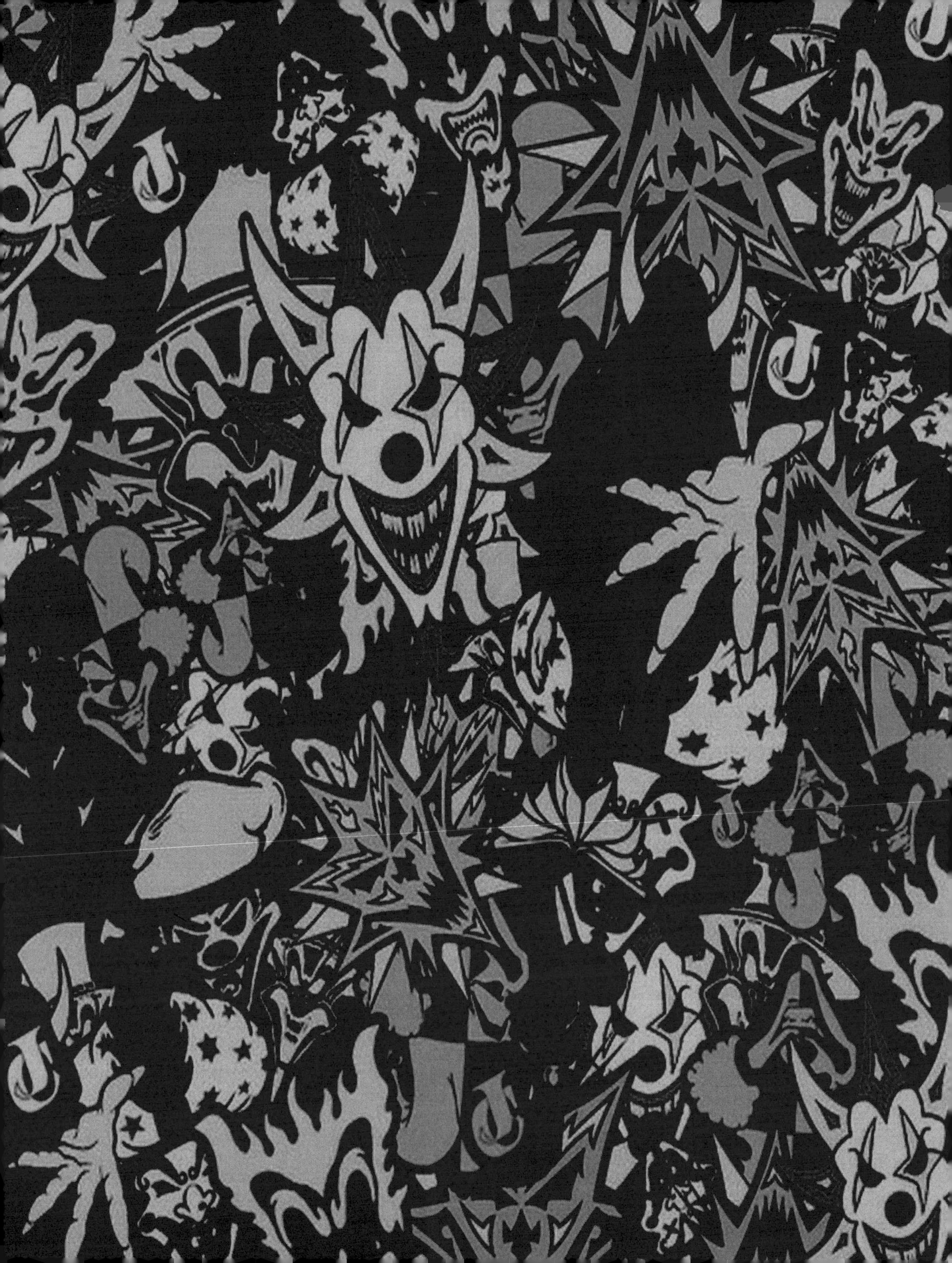

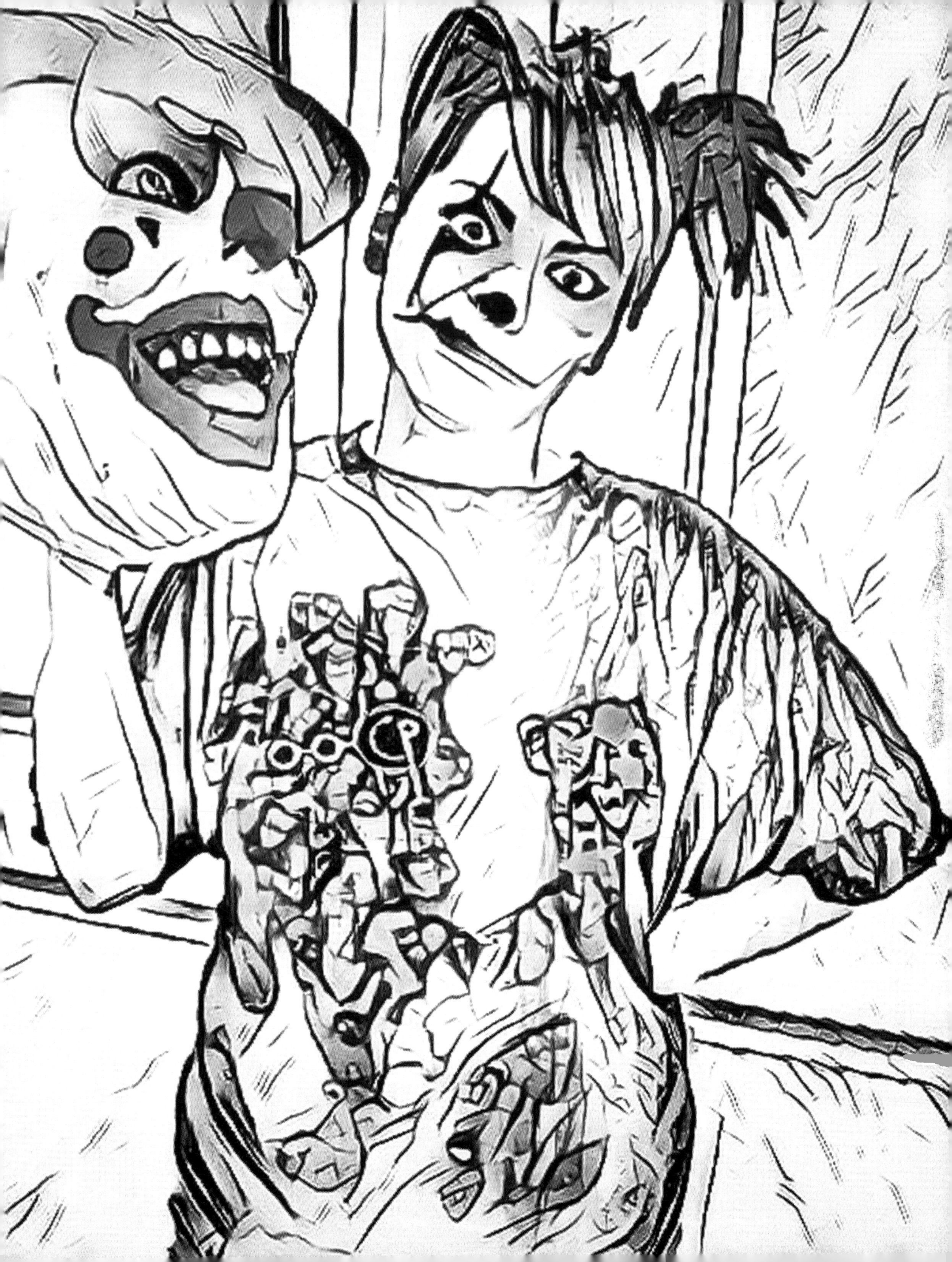

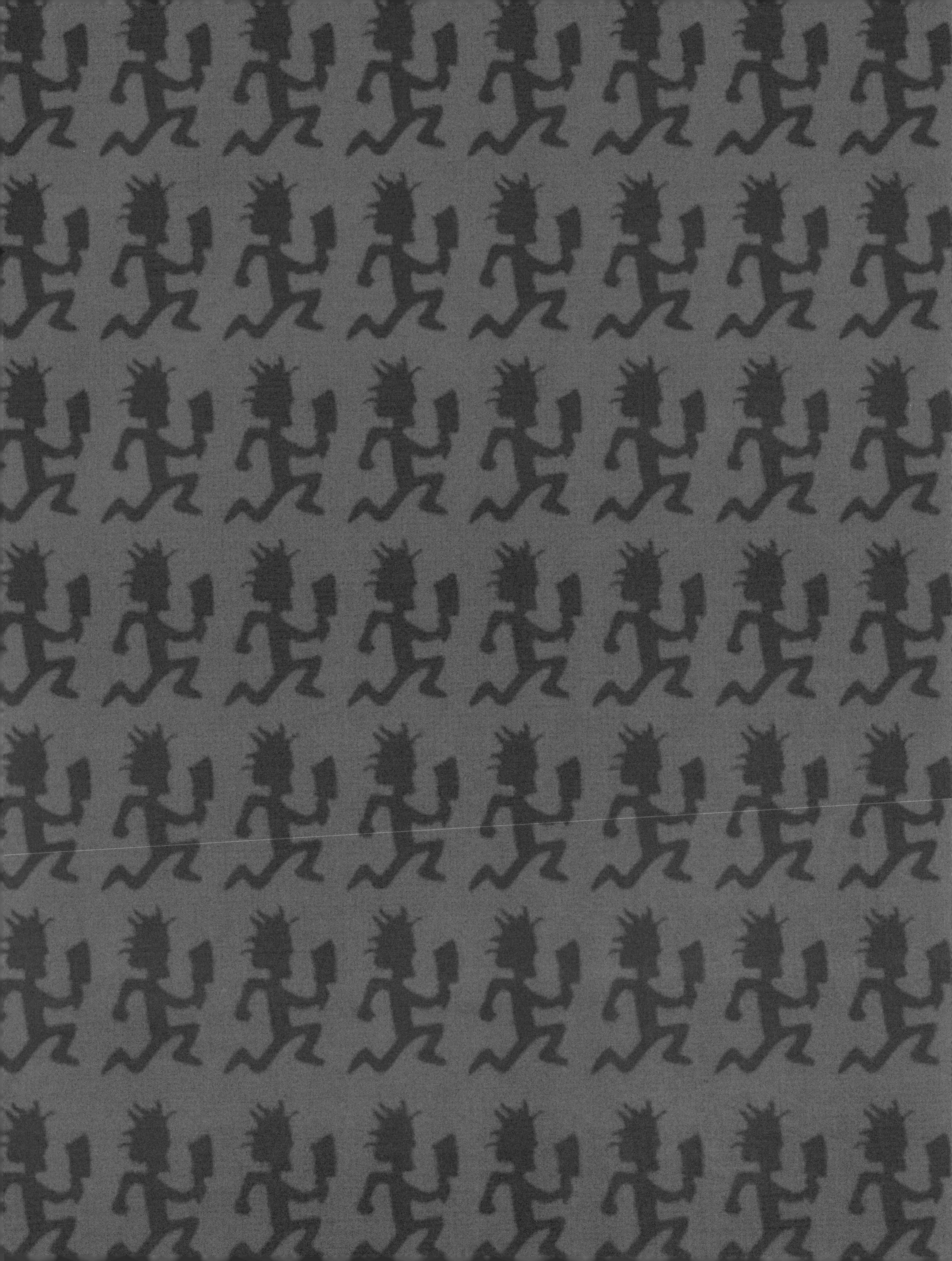

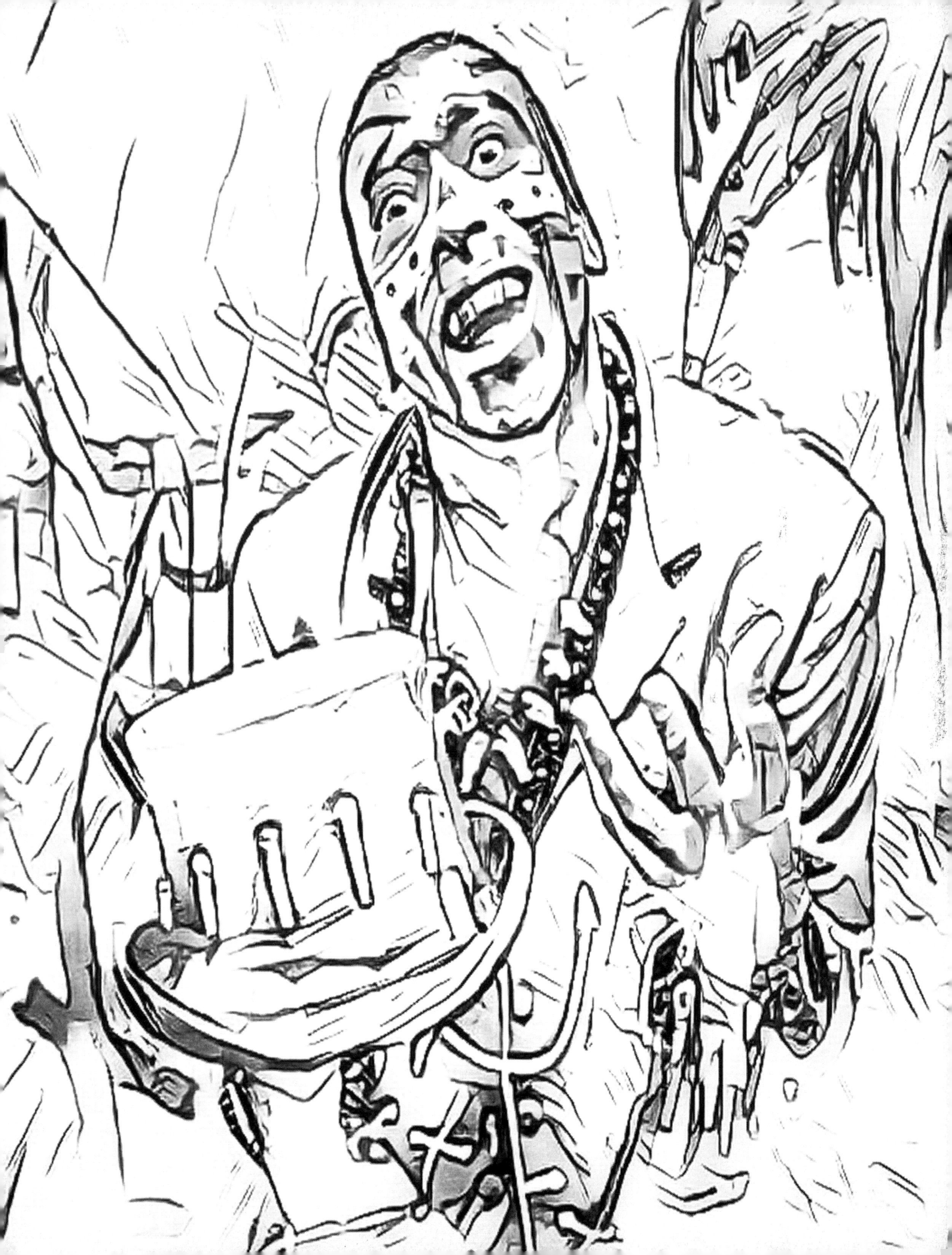

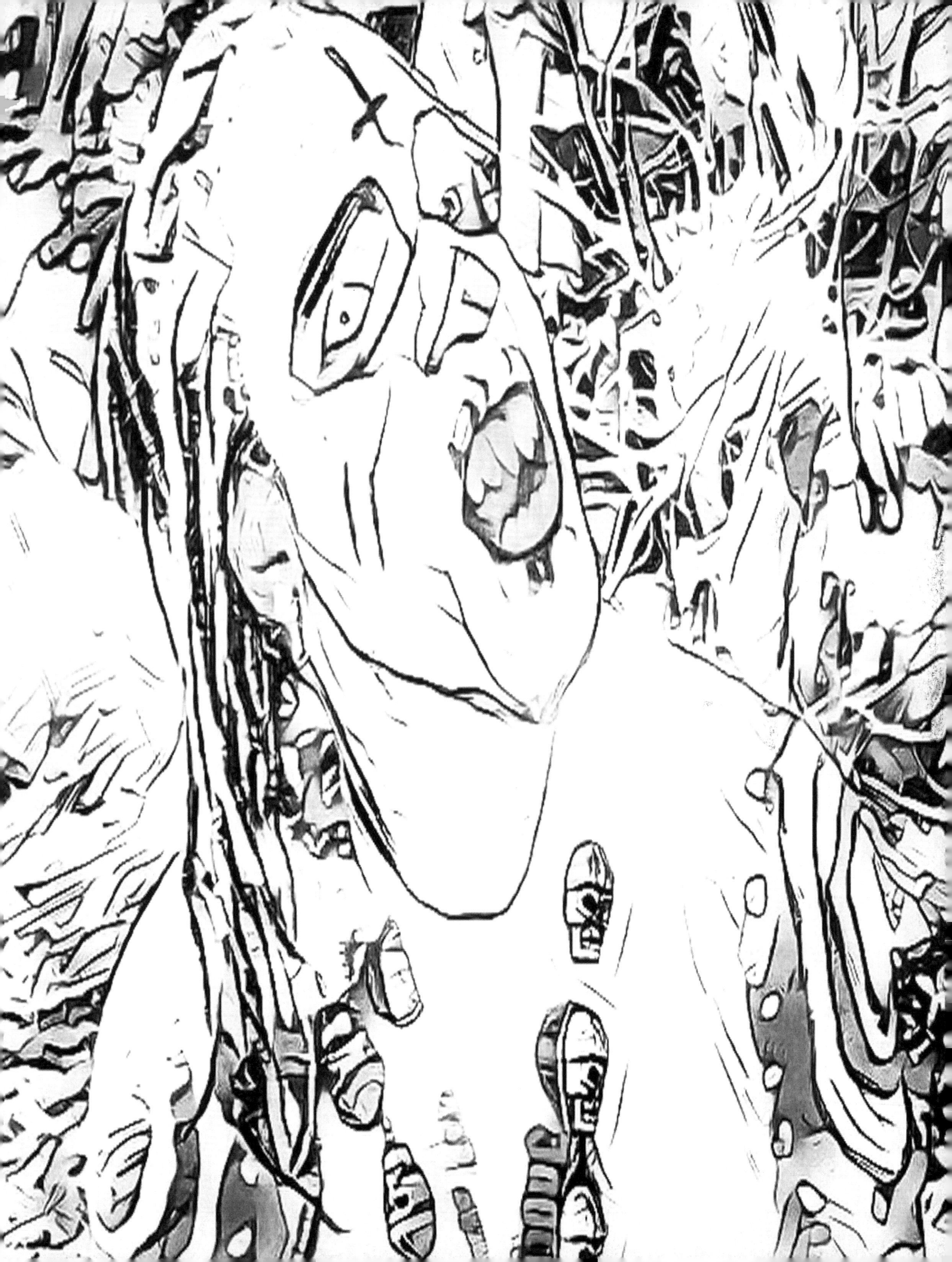

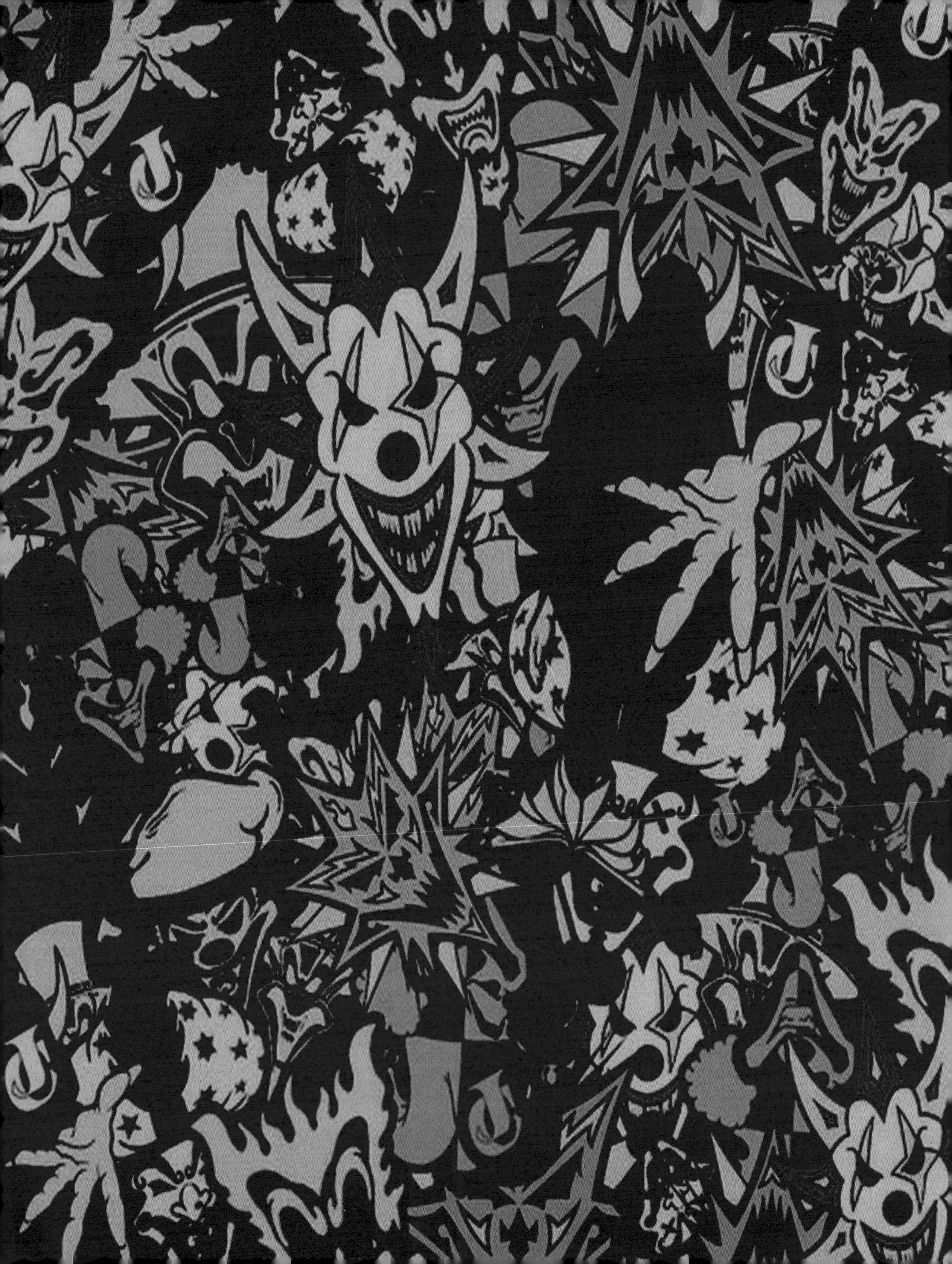

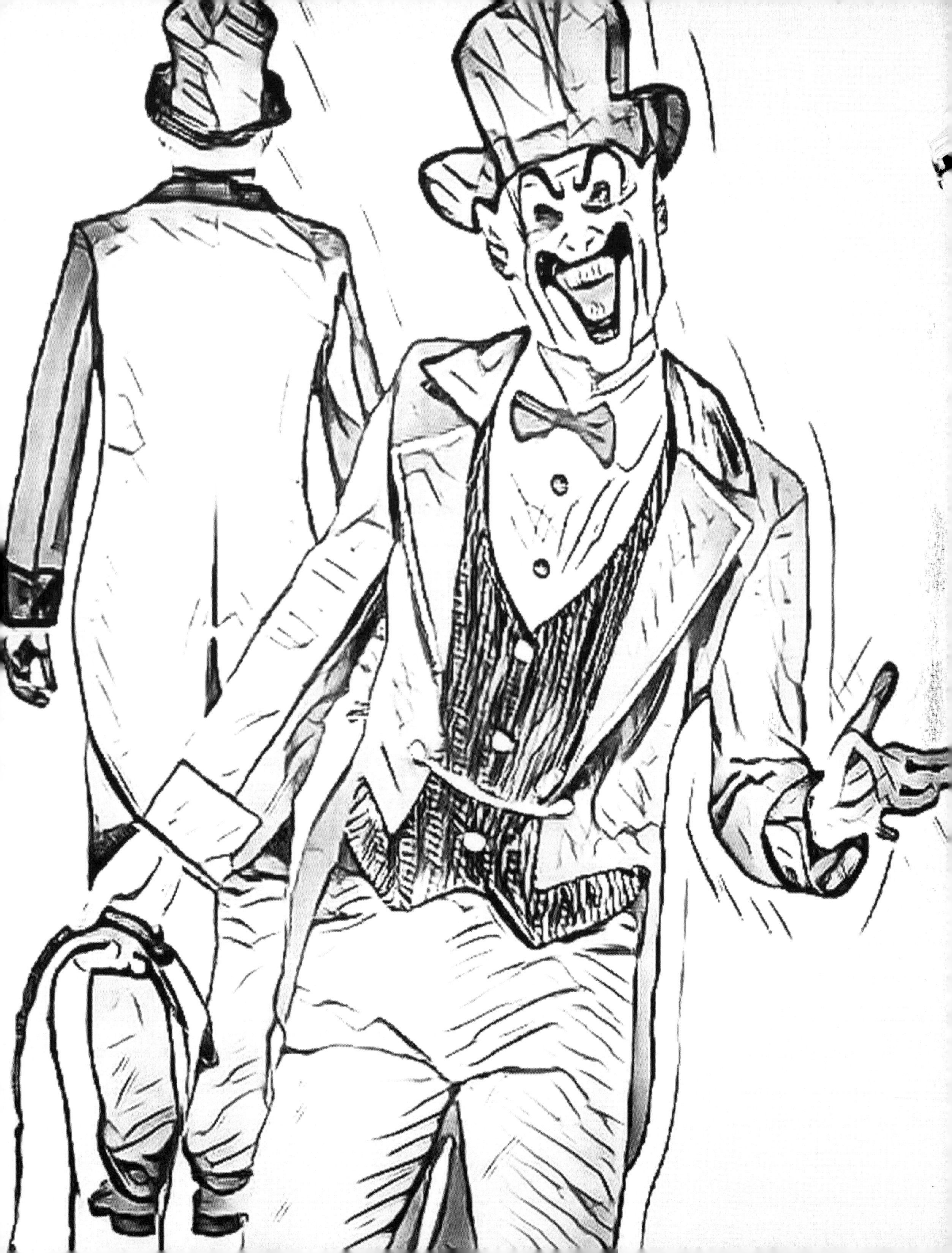

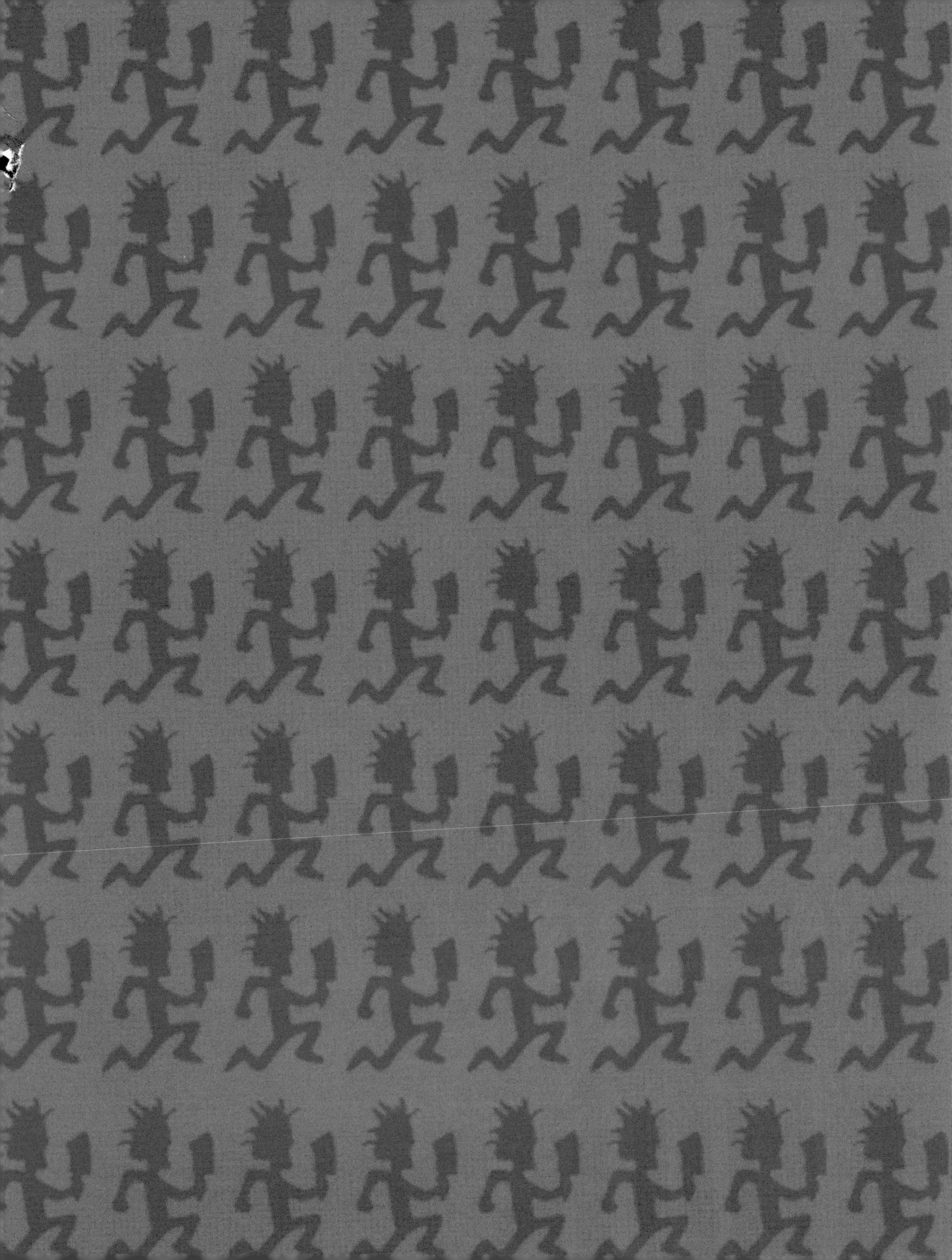

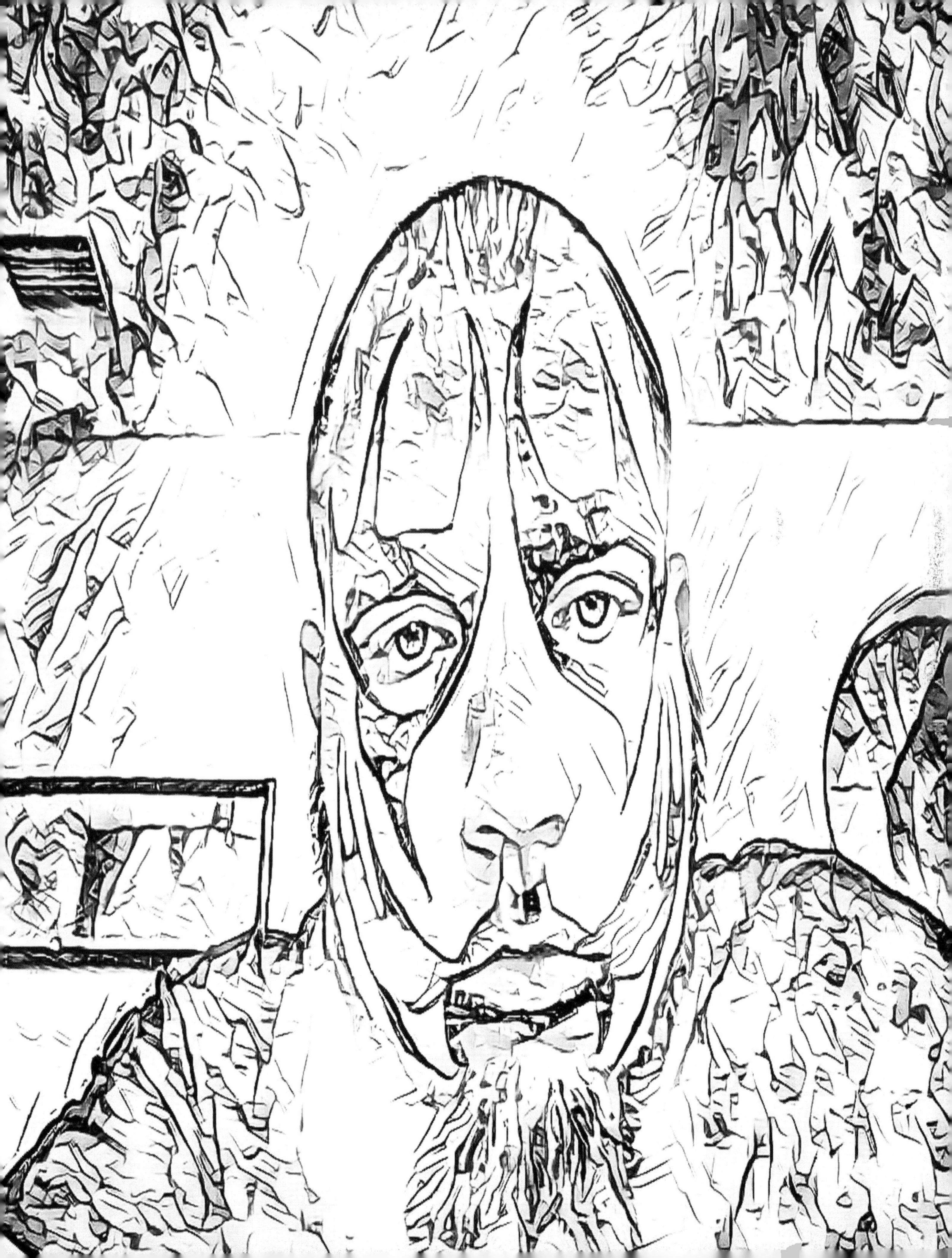

INSANE CLOWN POSSE

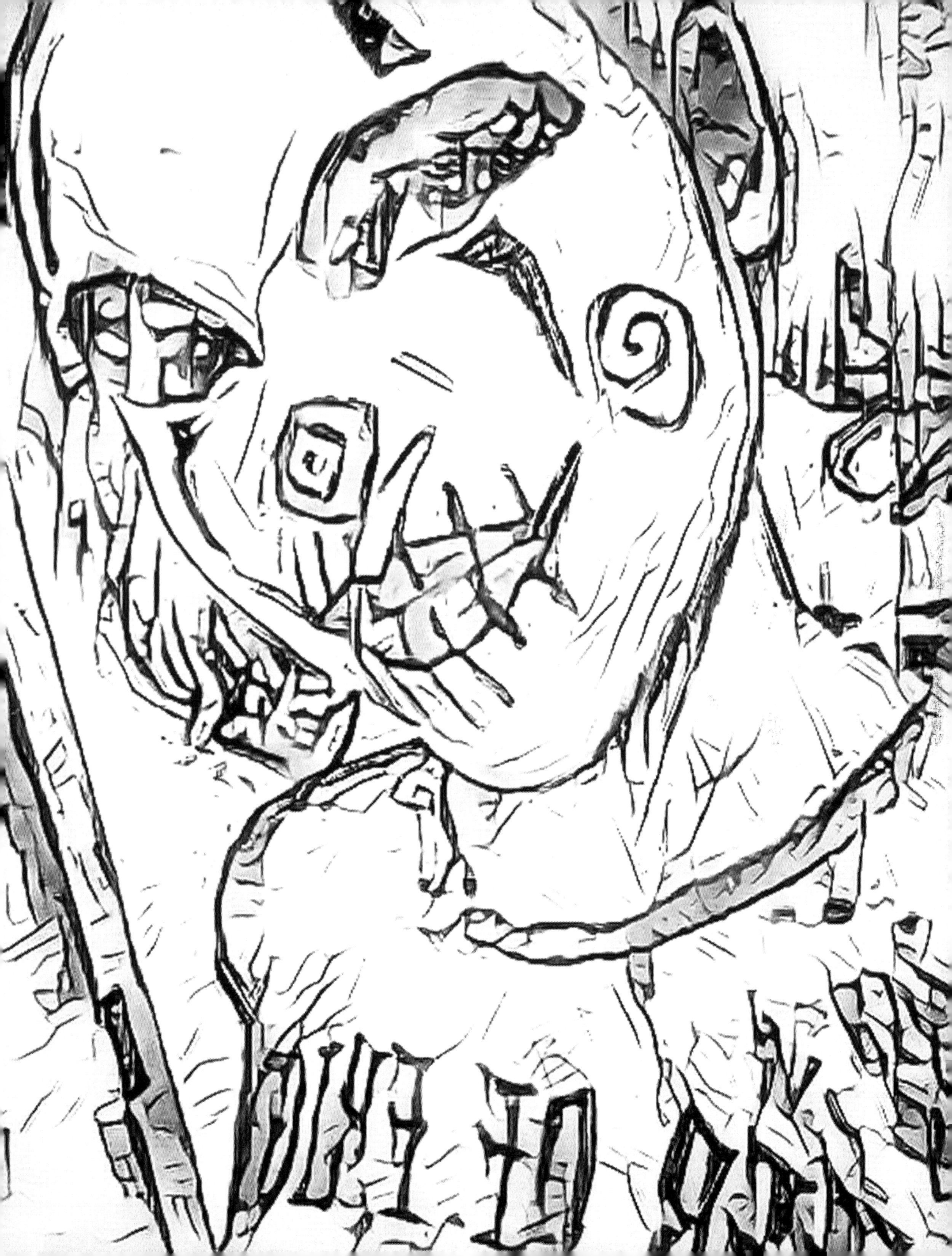

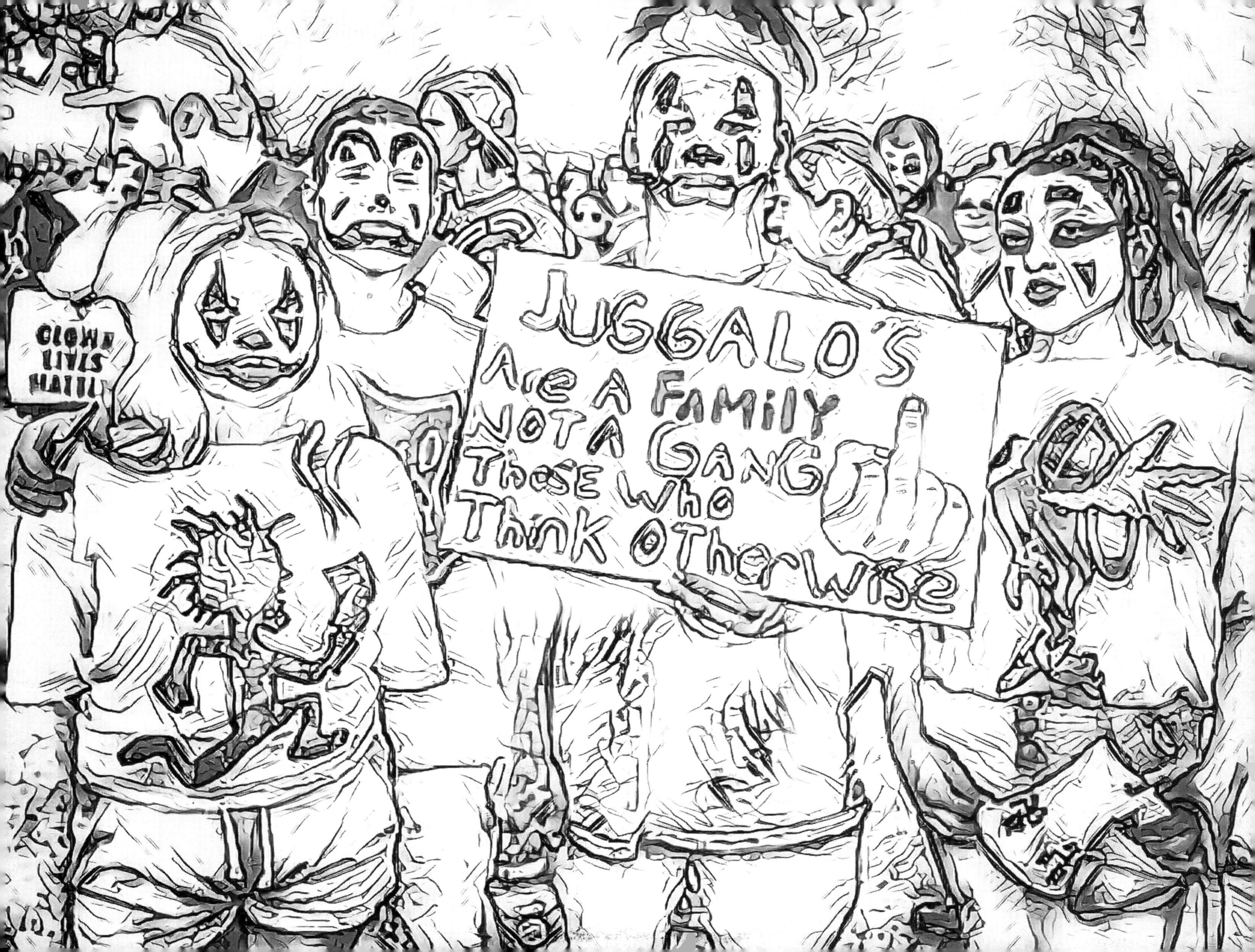

JUGGALO'S
ARE A FAMILY
NOT A GANG
THOSE WHO
THINK OTHERWISE
CLOWN LIVES MATTER

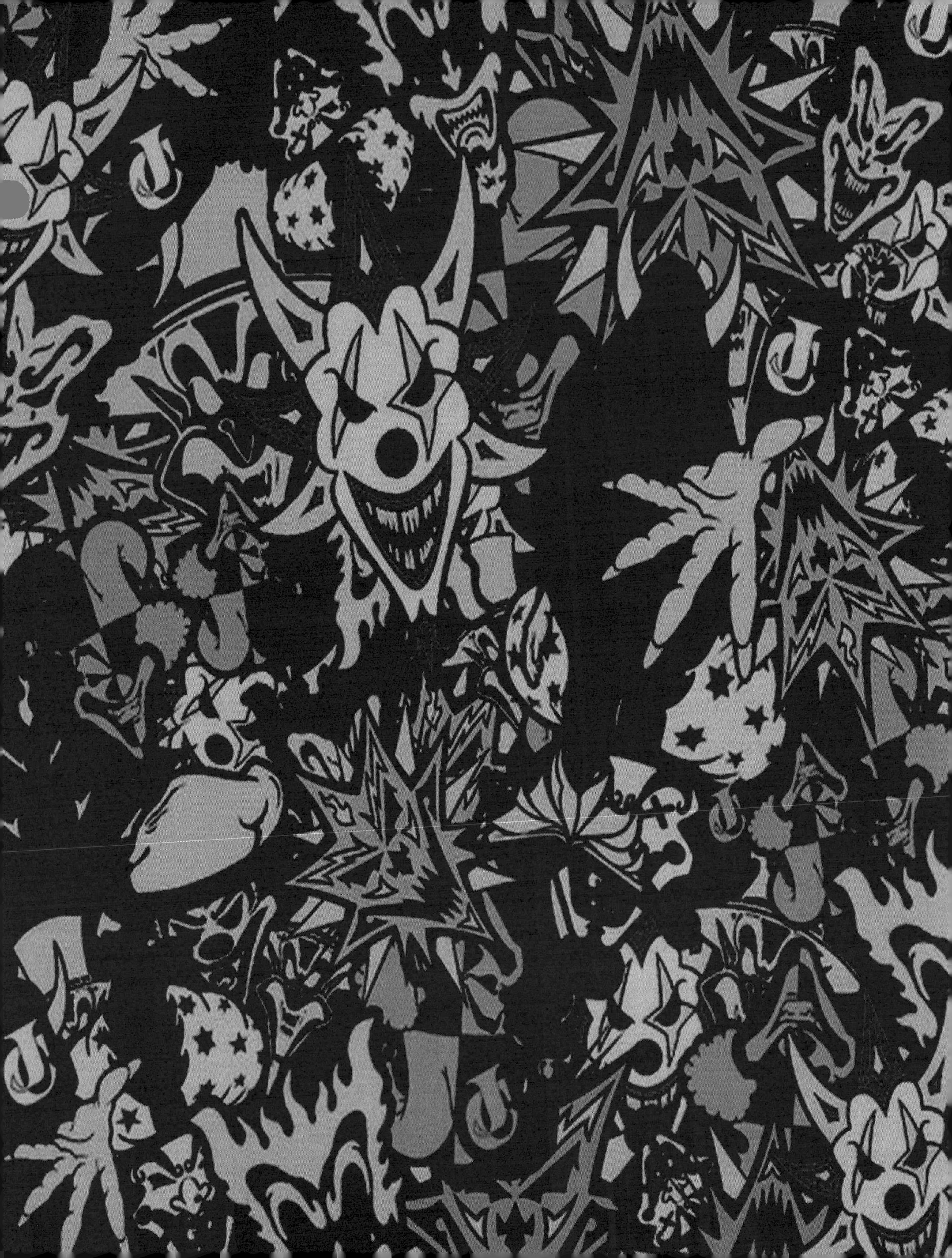

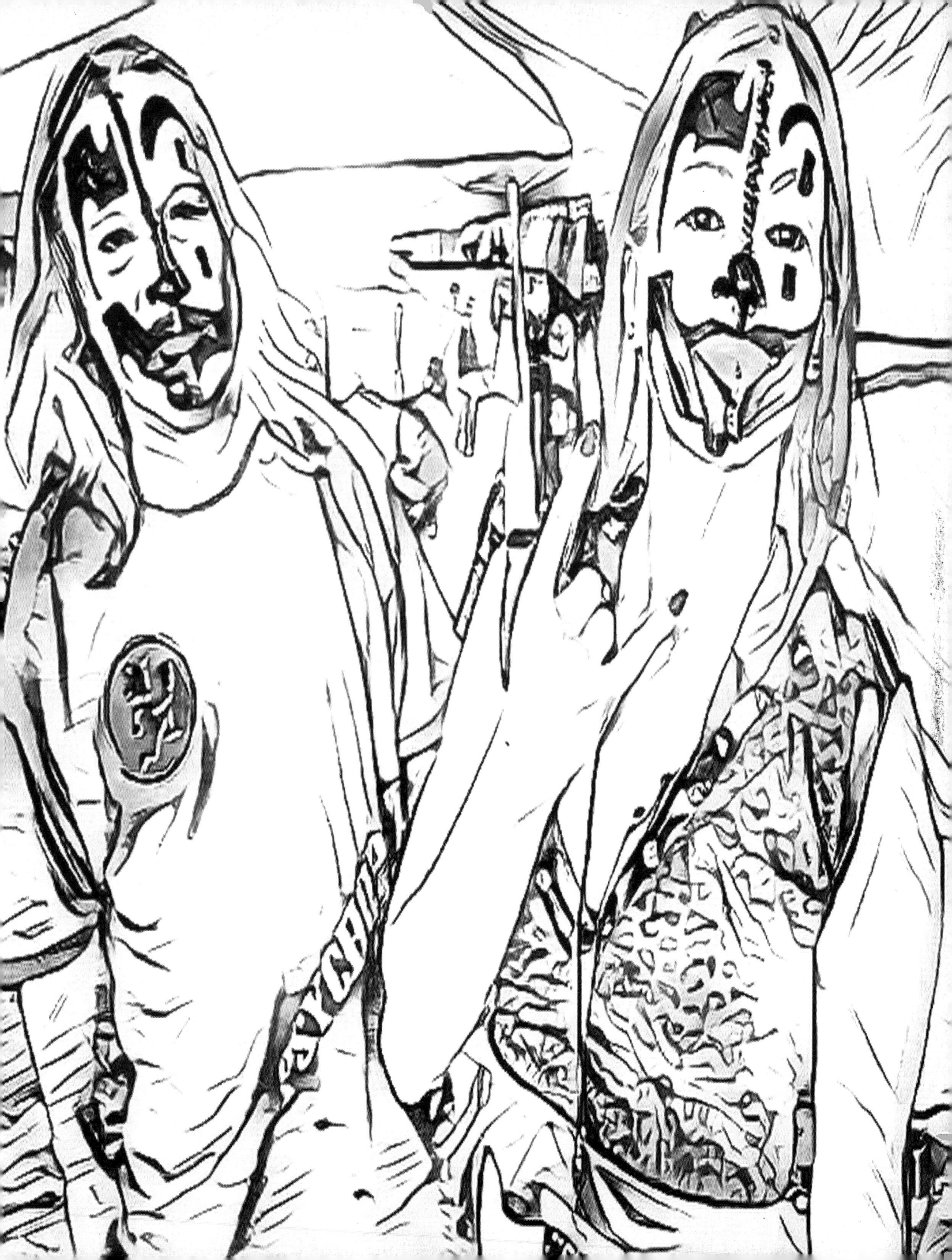

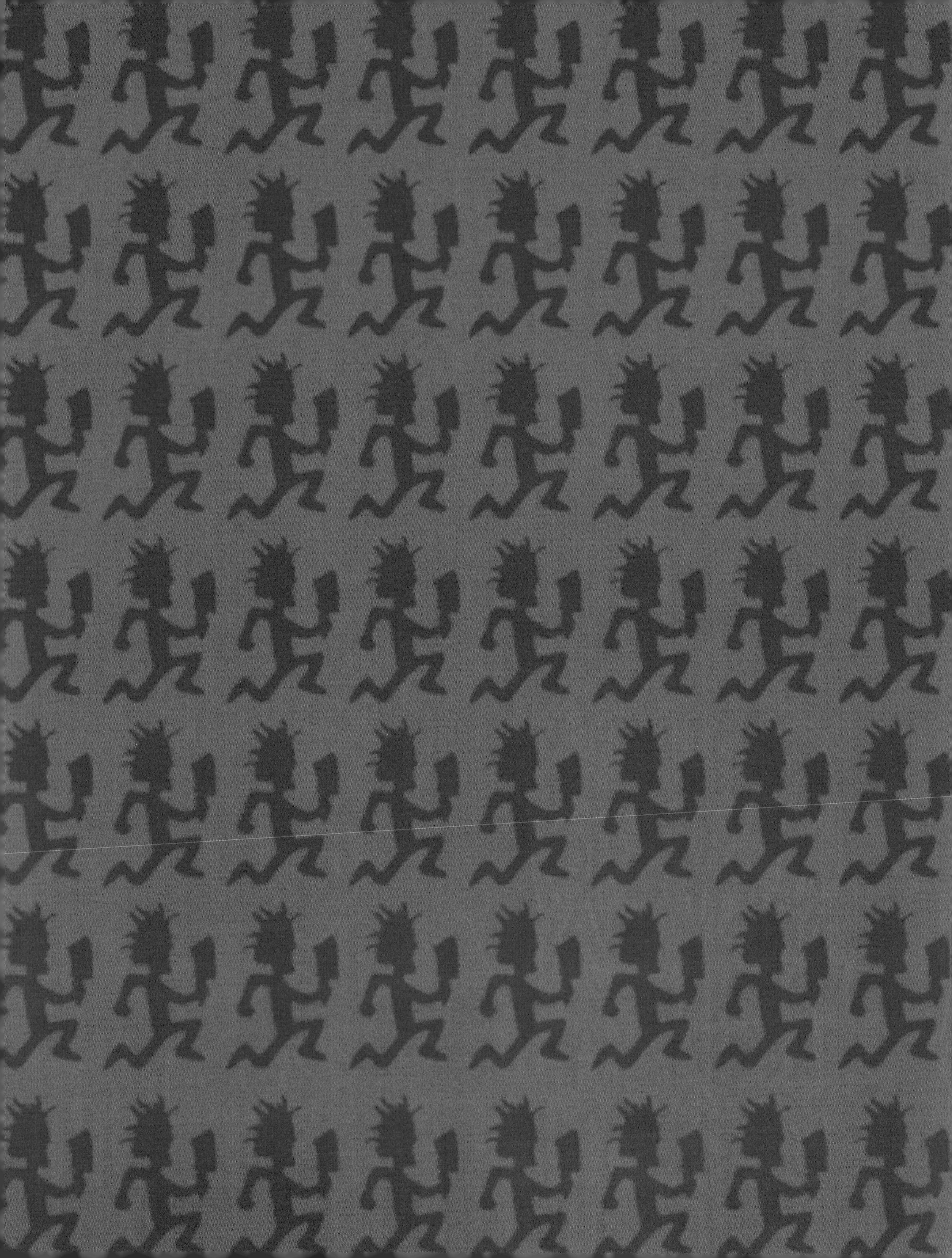

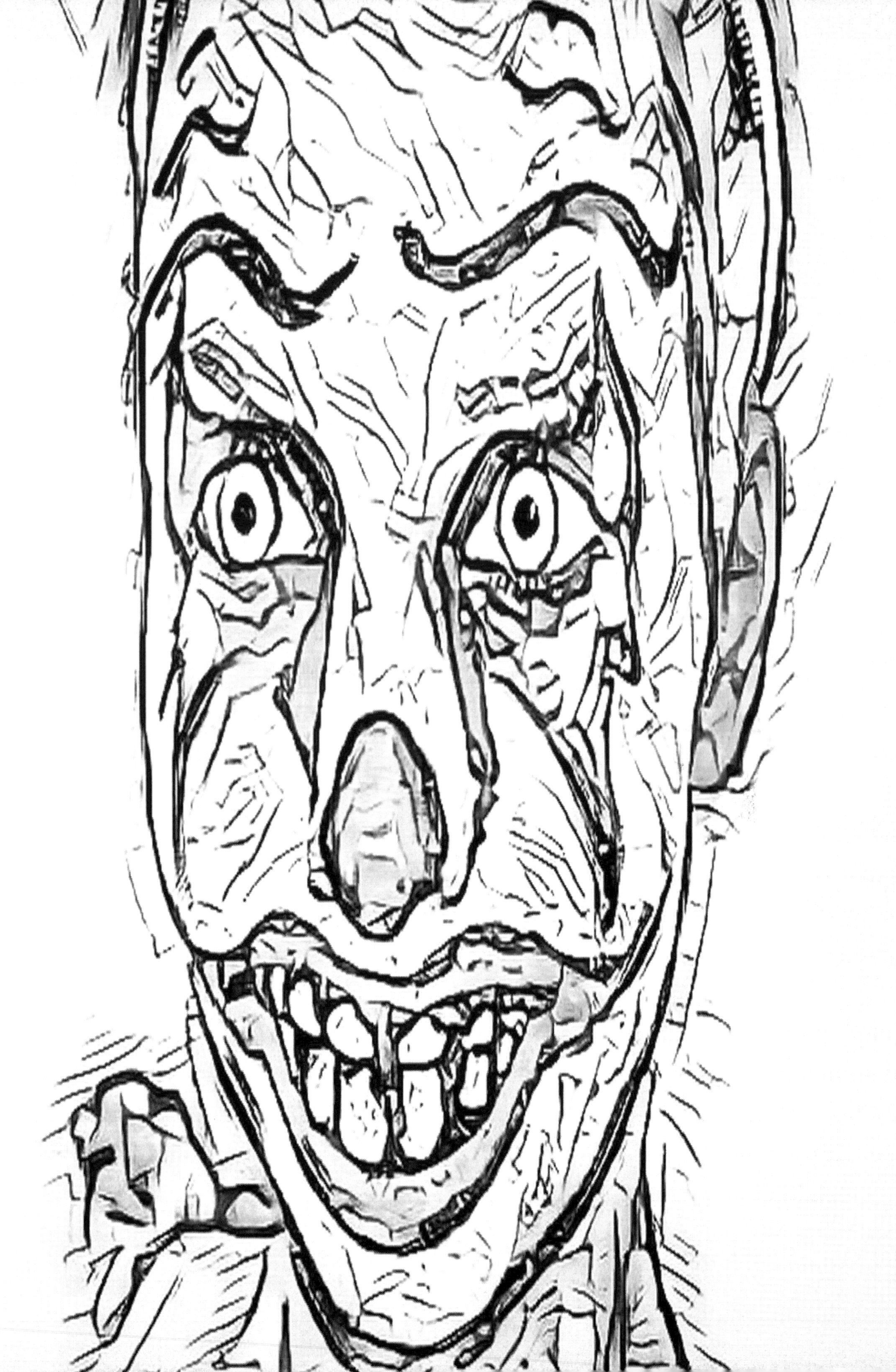

INSANE CLOWN POSSE

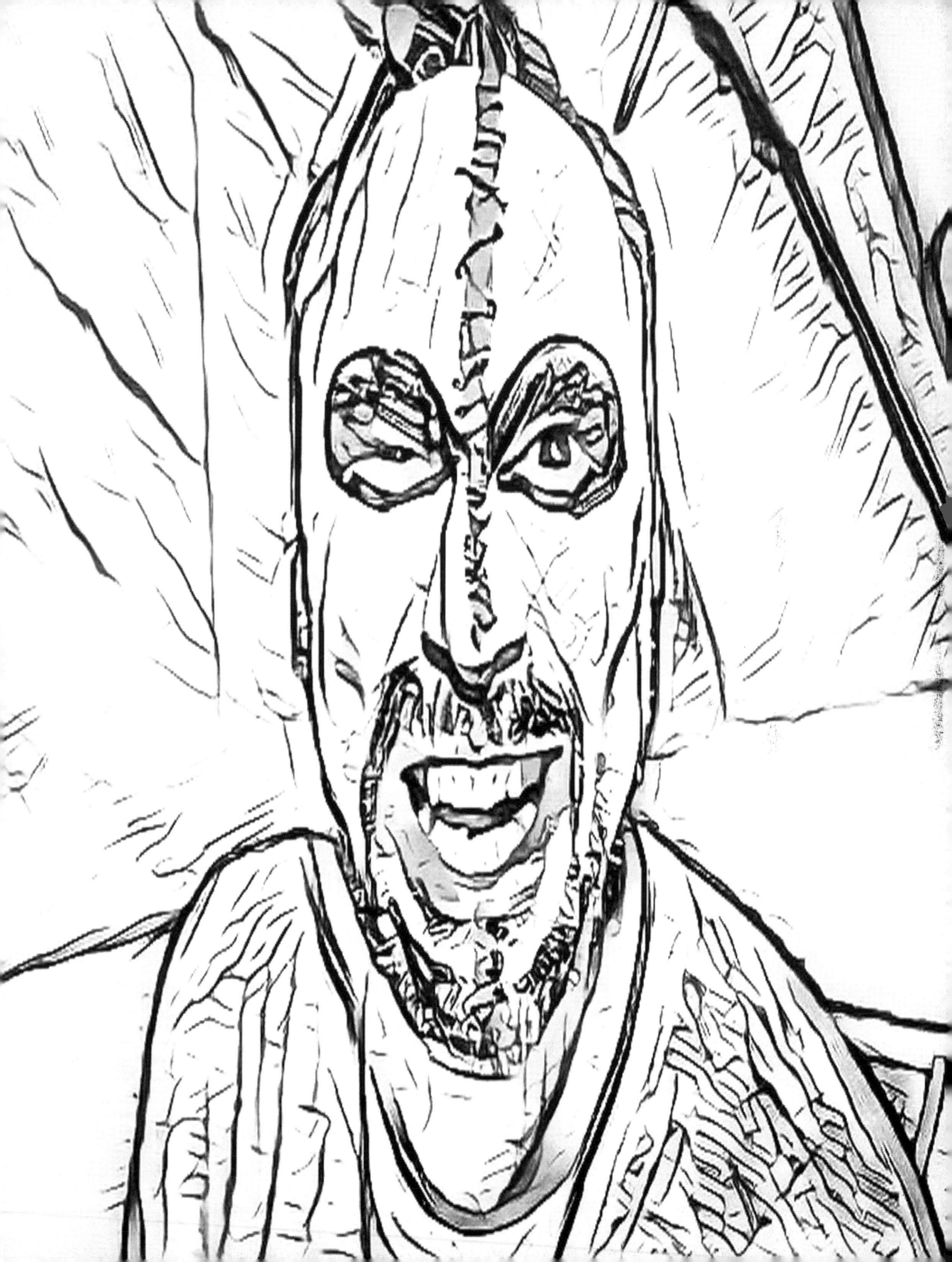

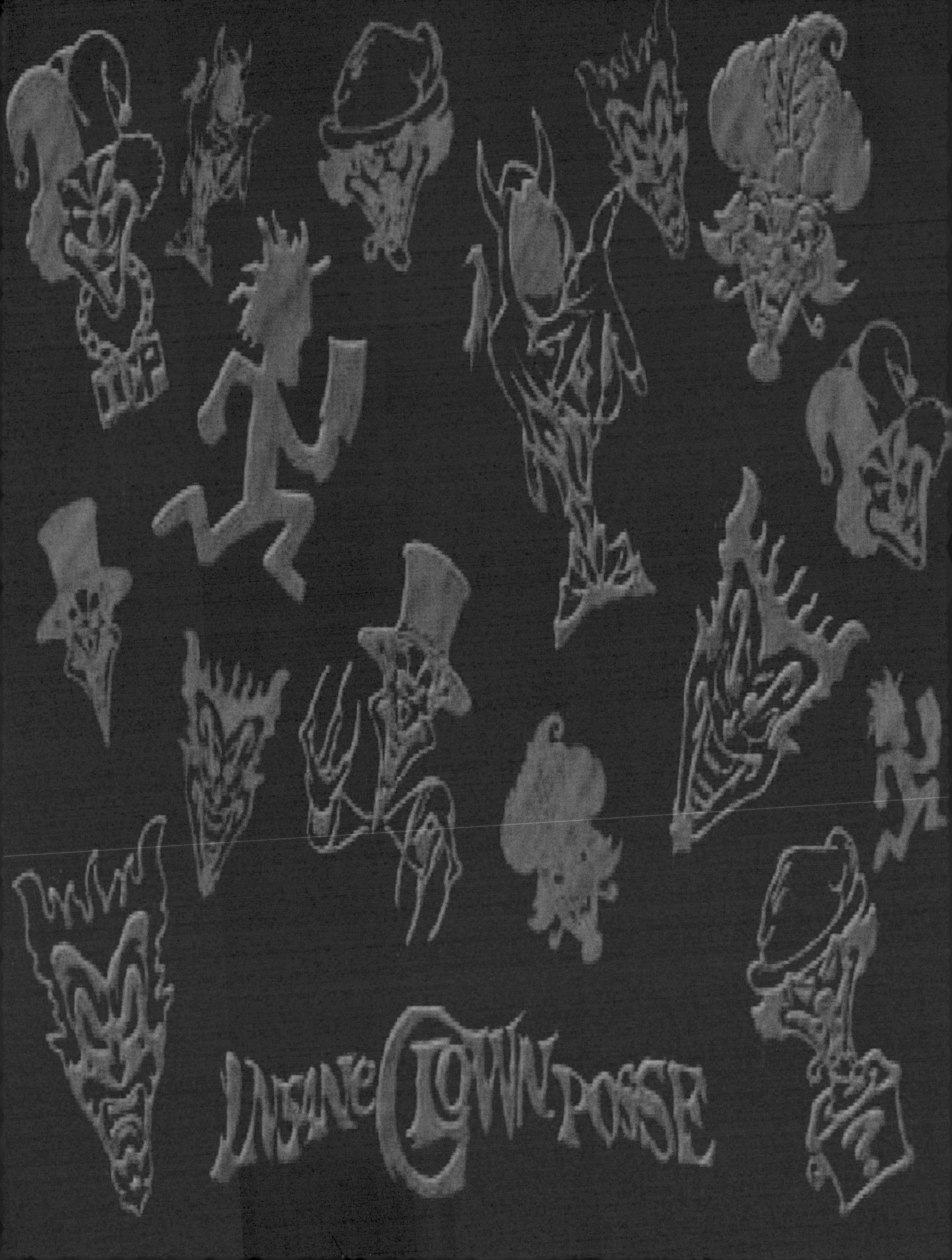

INSANE CLOWN POSSE

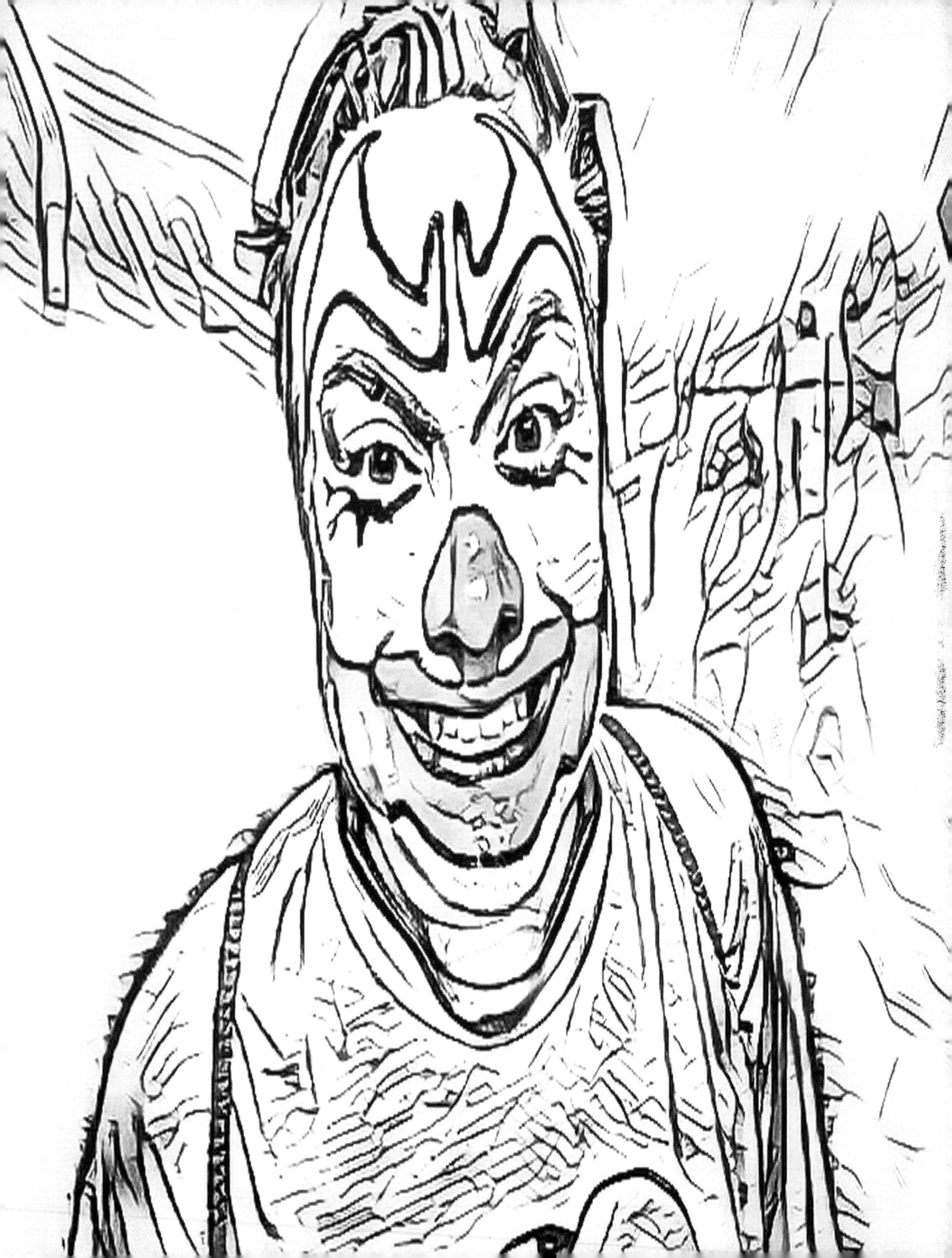

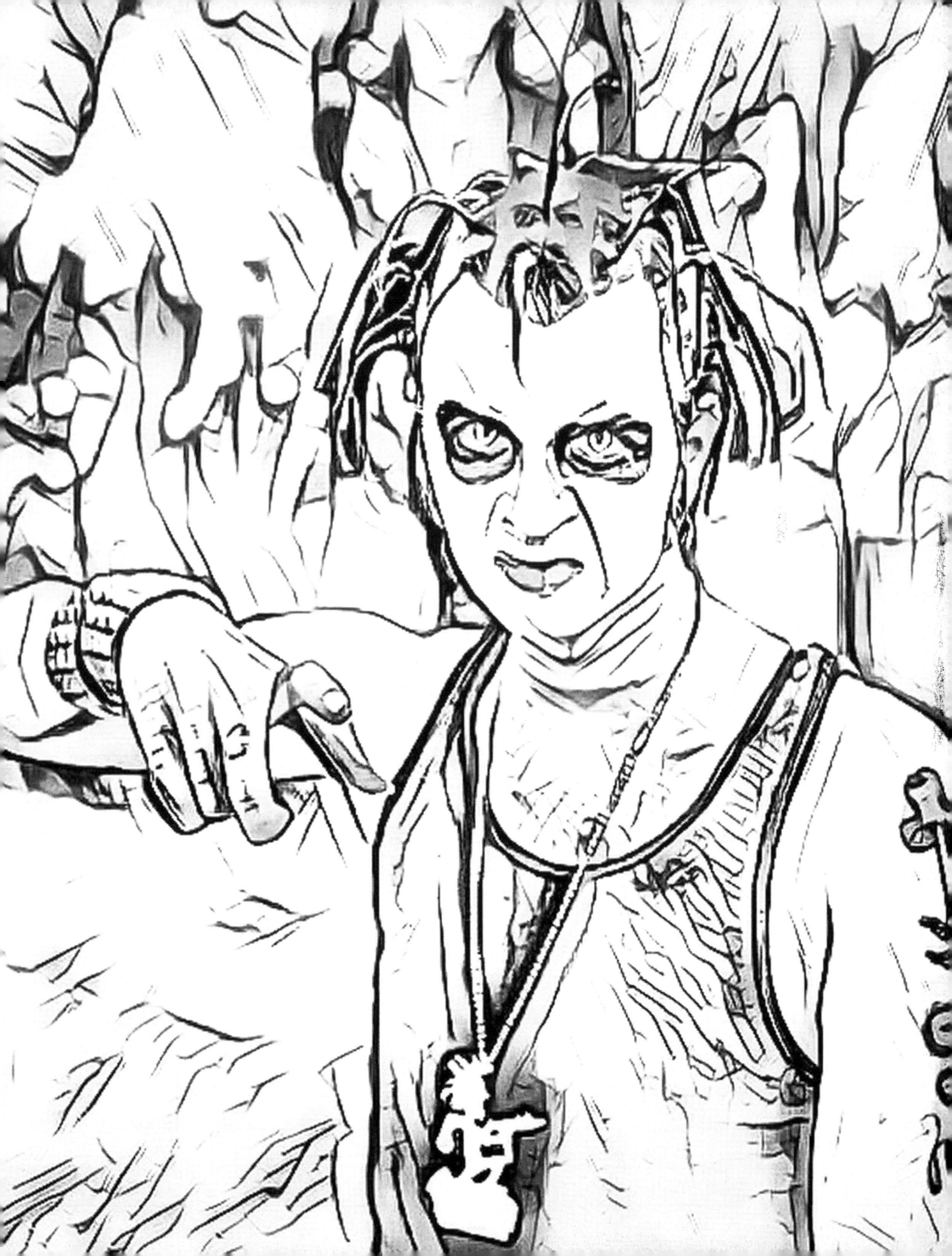

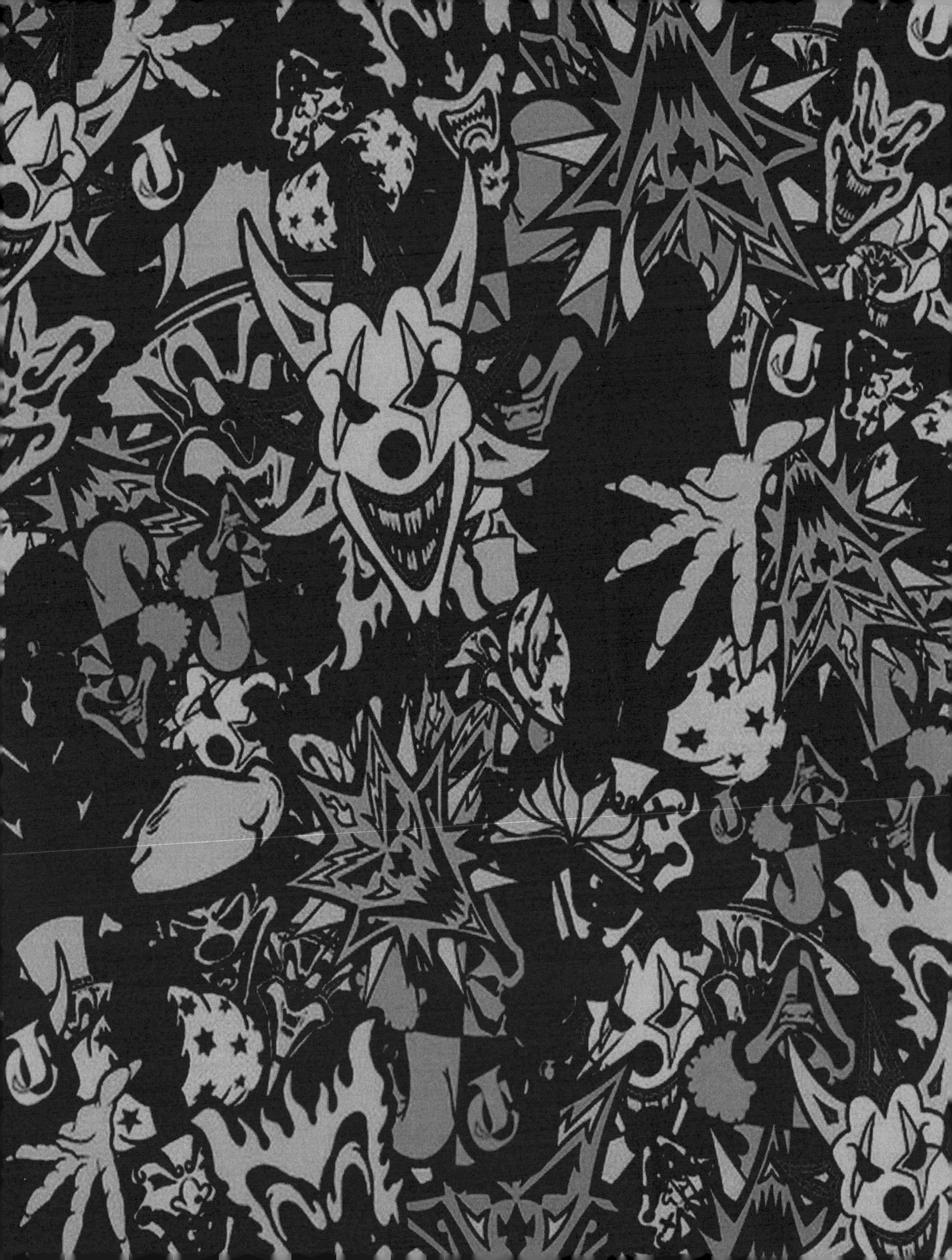

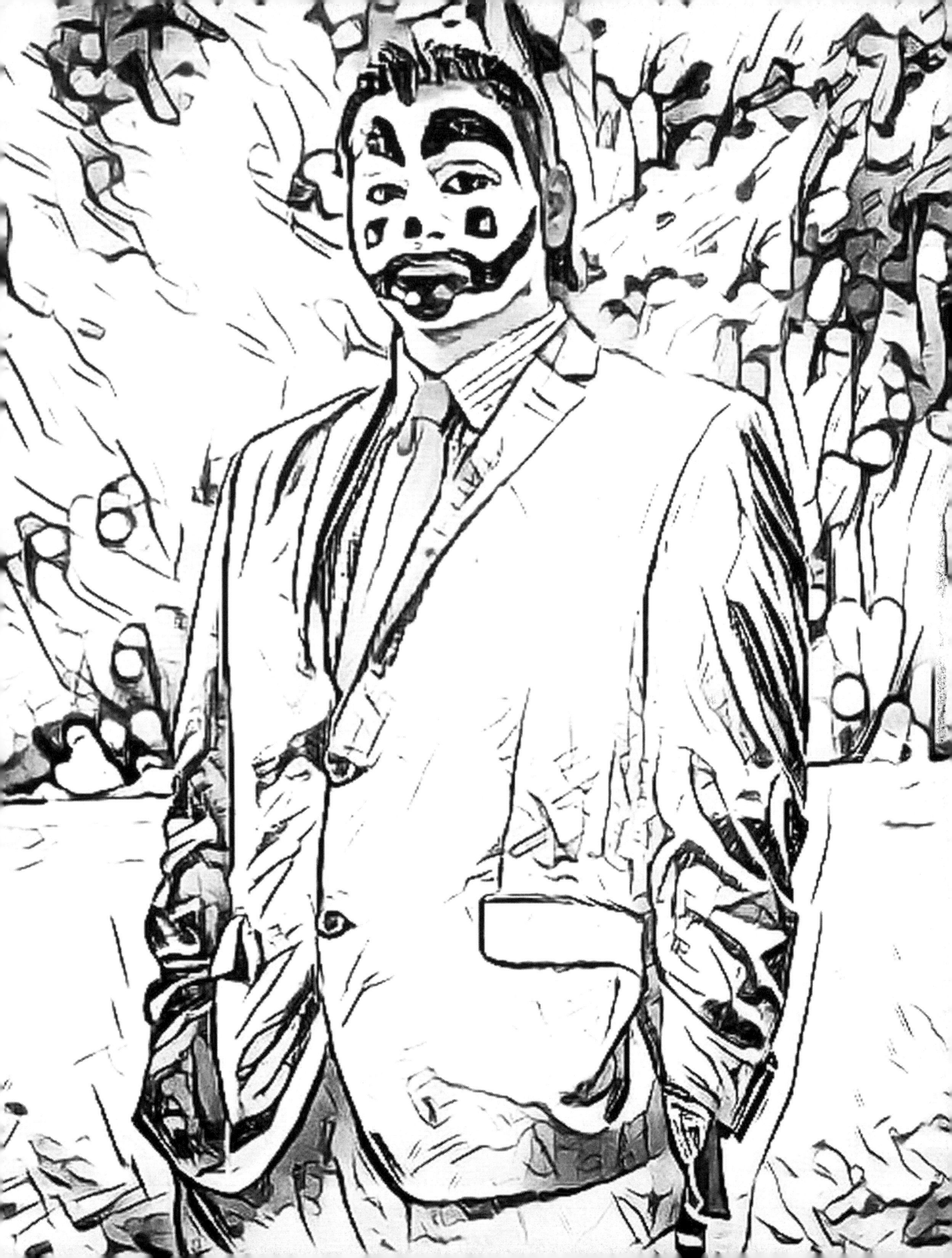

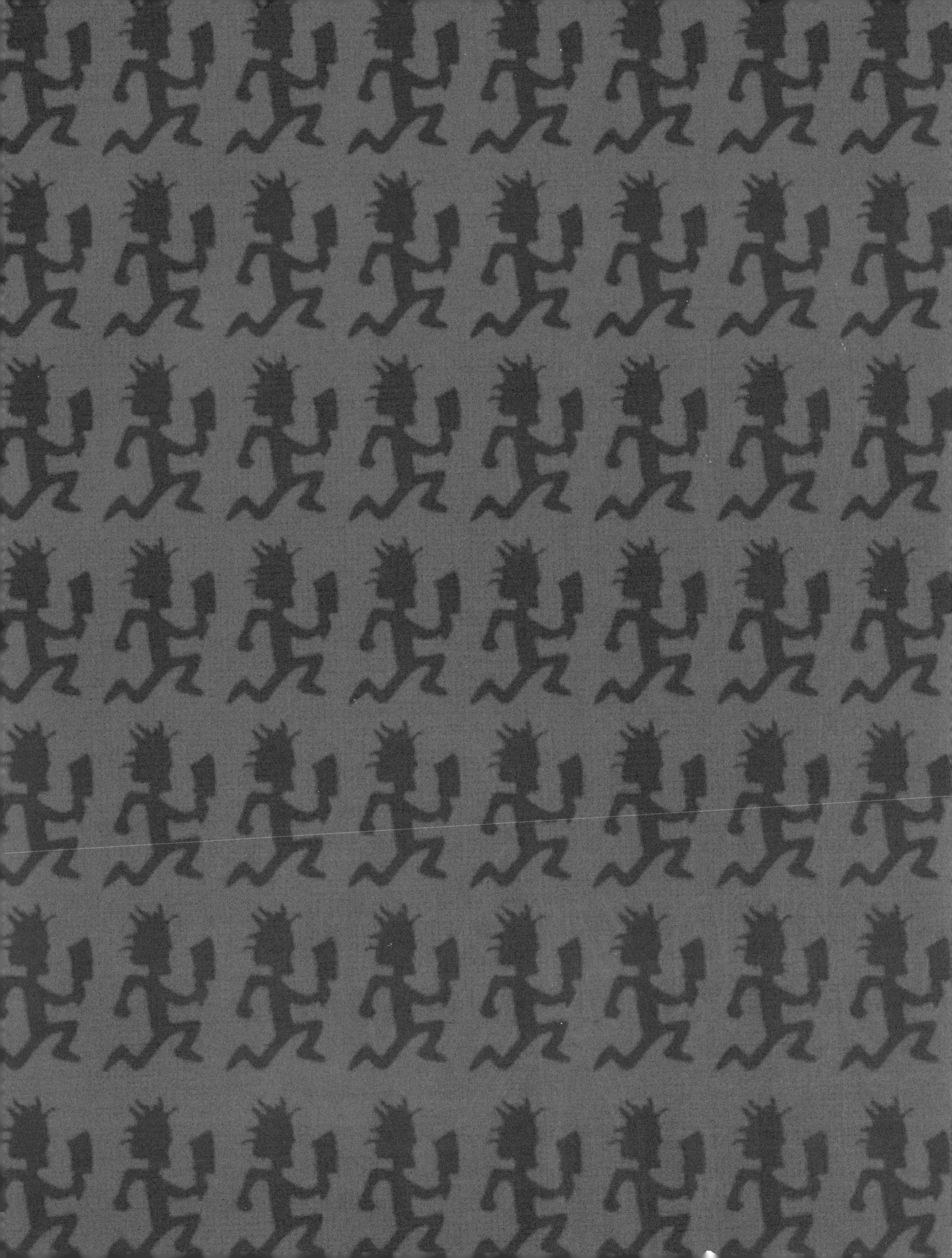

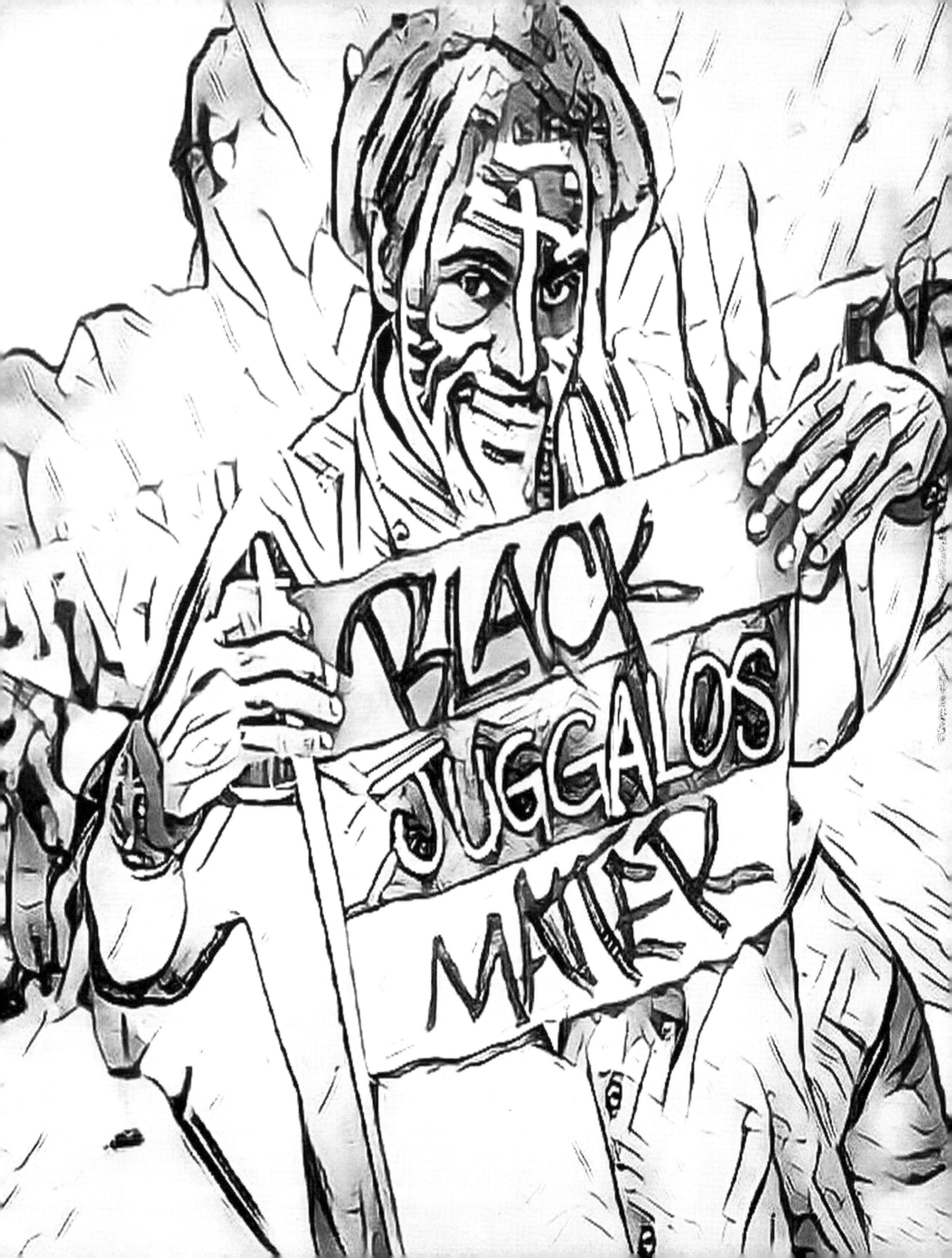

BLACK
JUGGALOS
MATTER

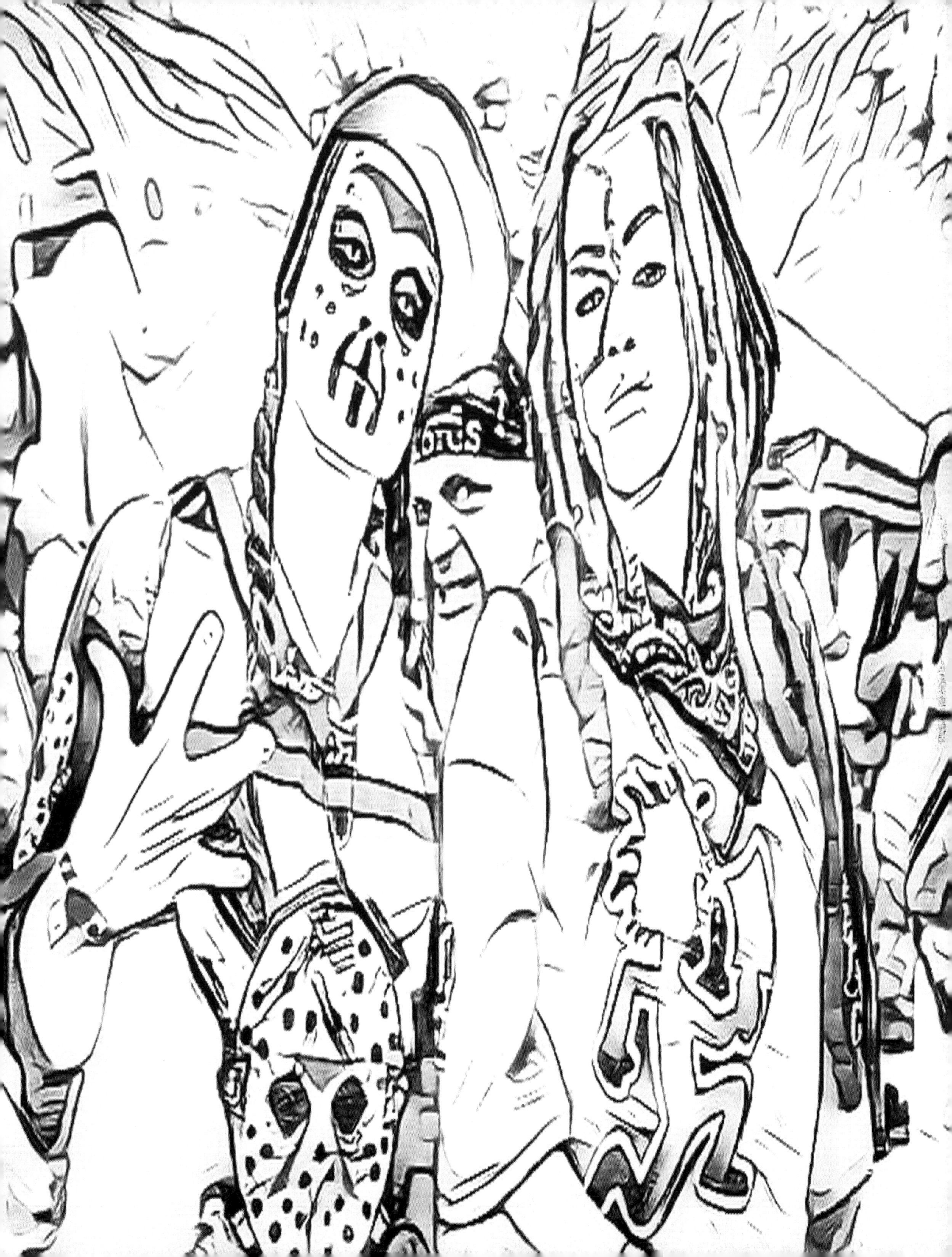

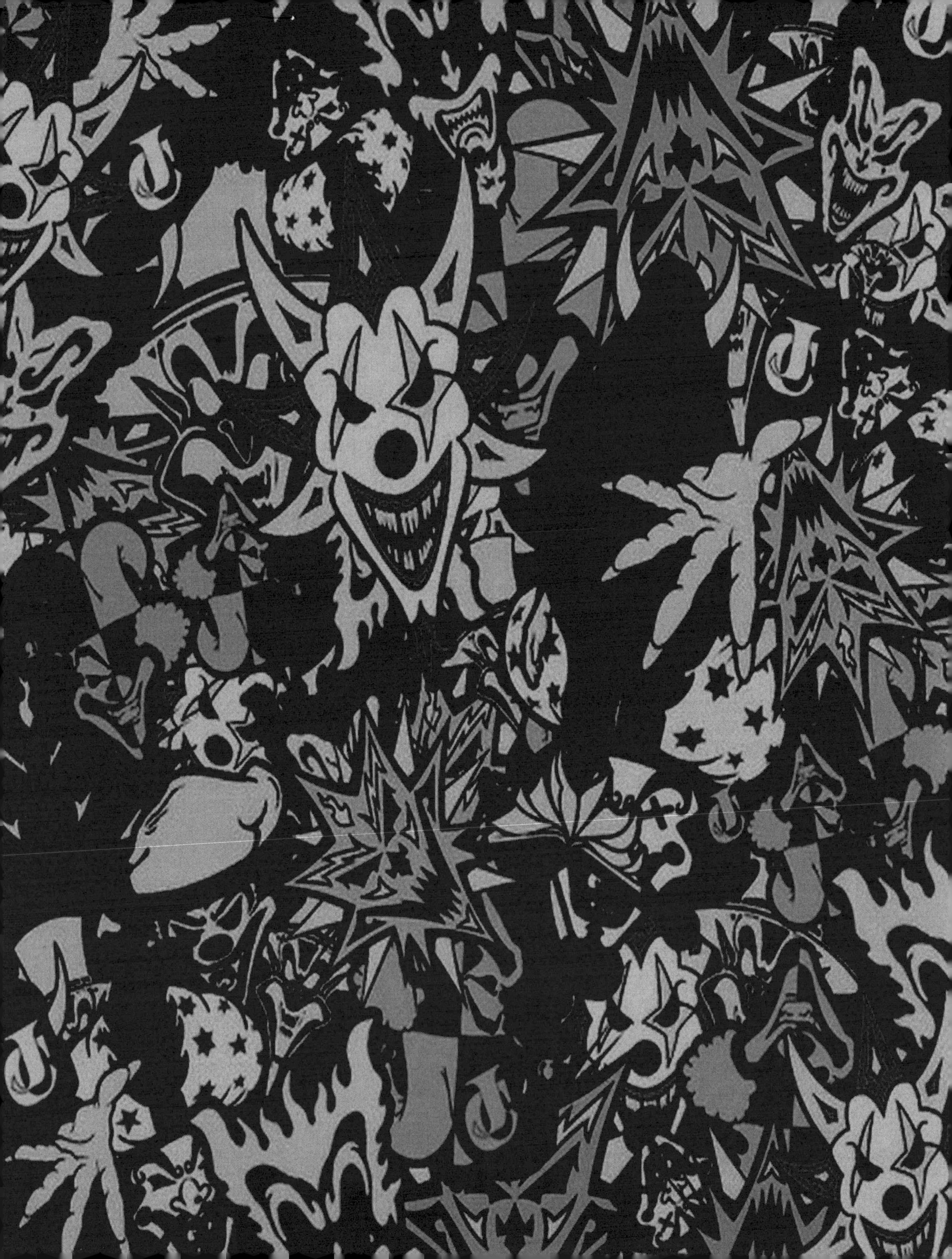

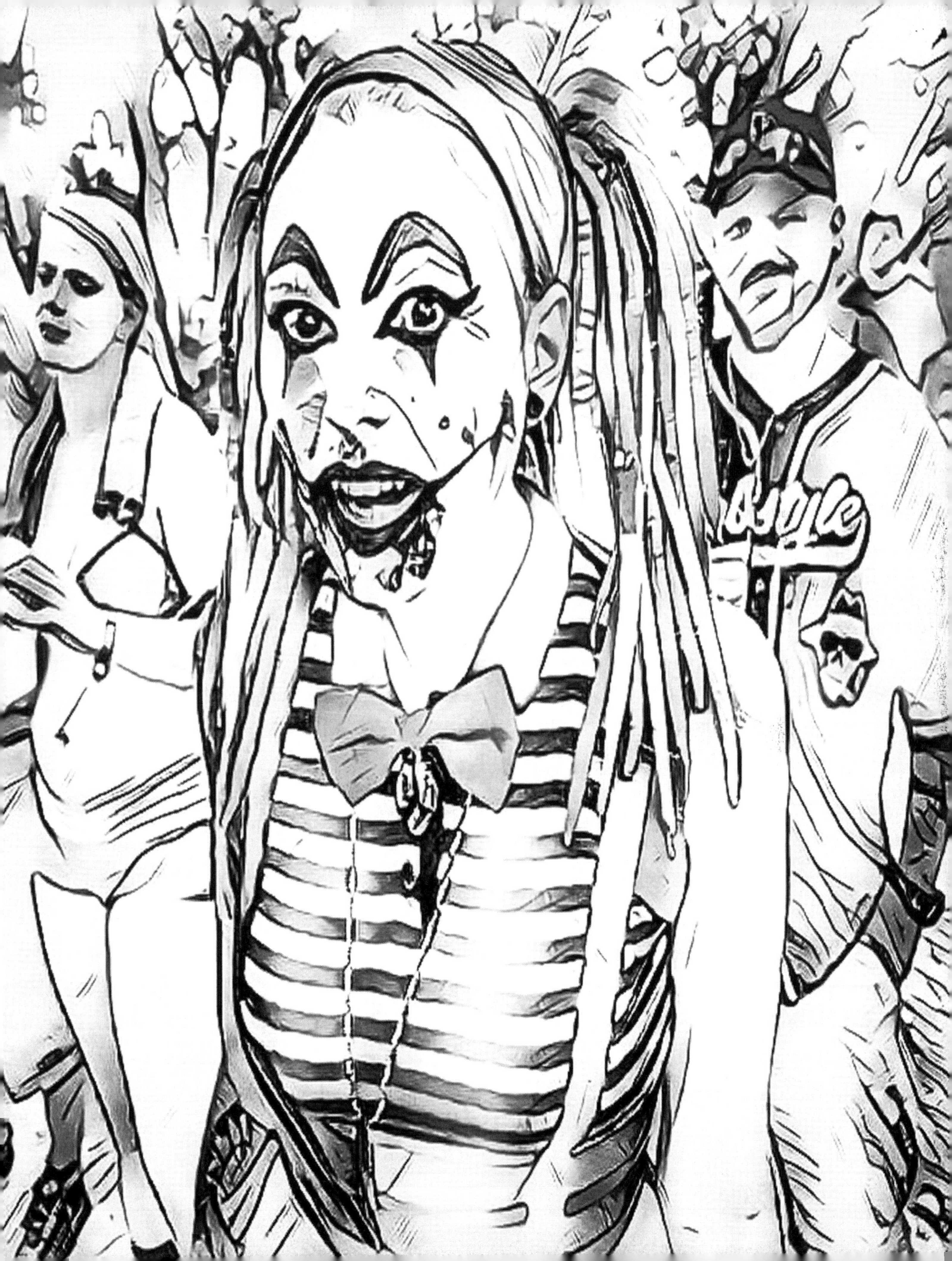

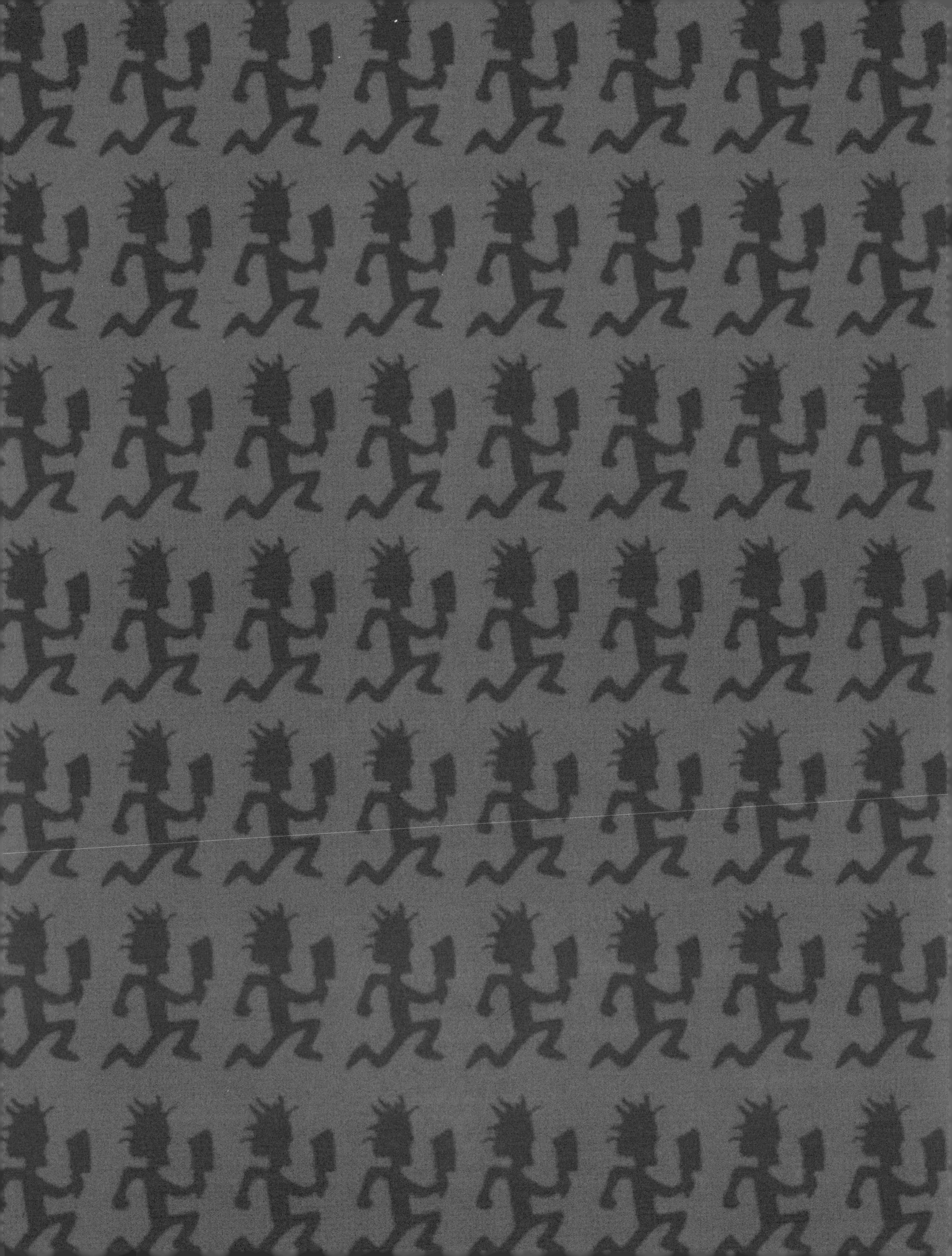

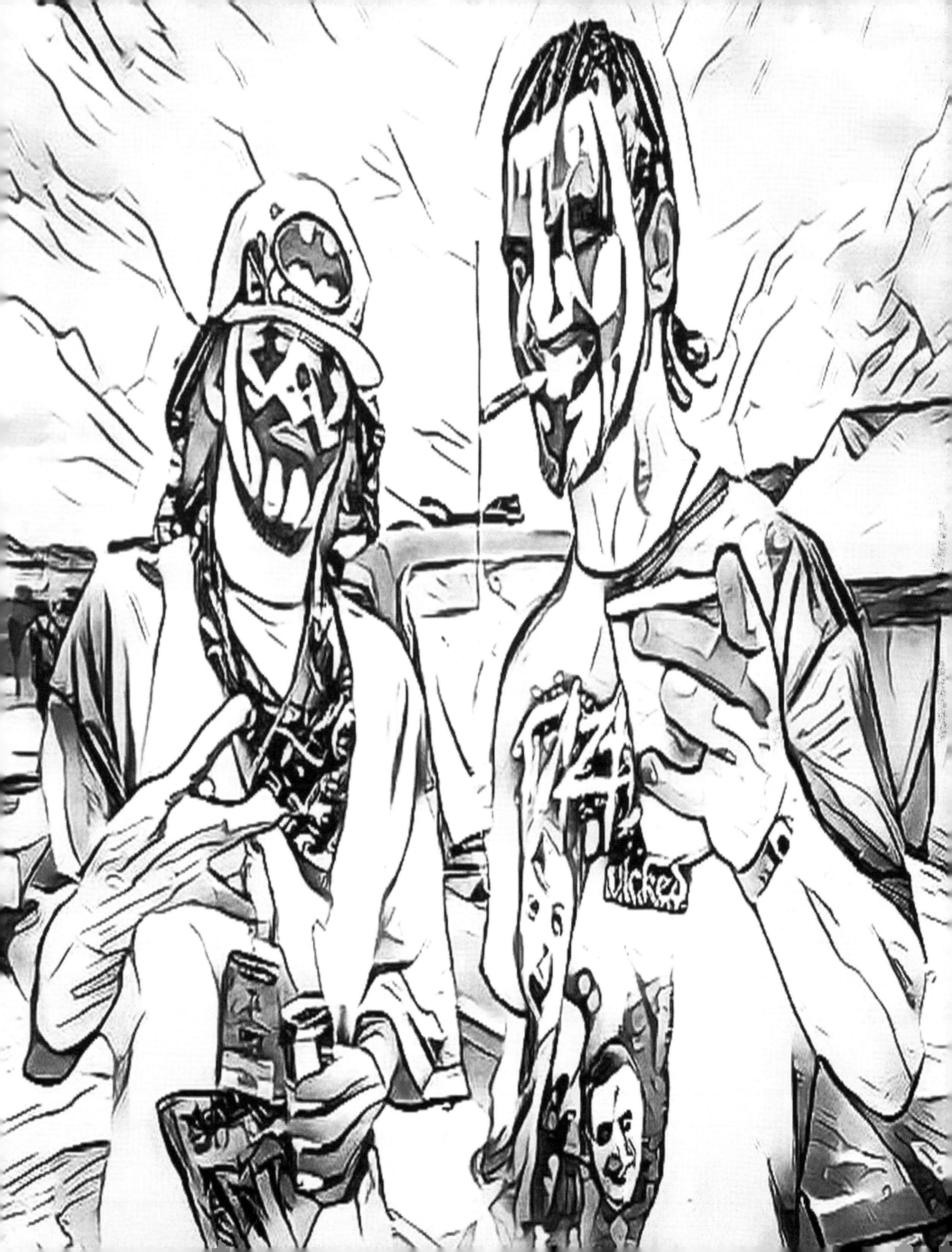

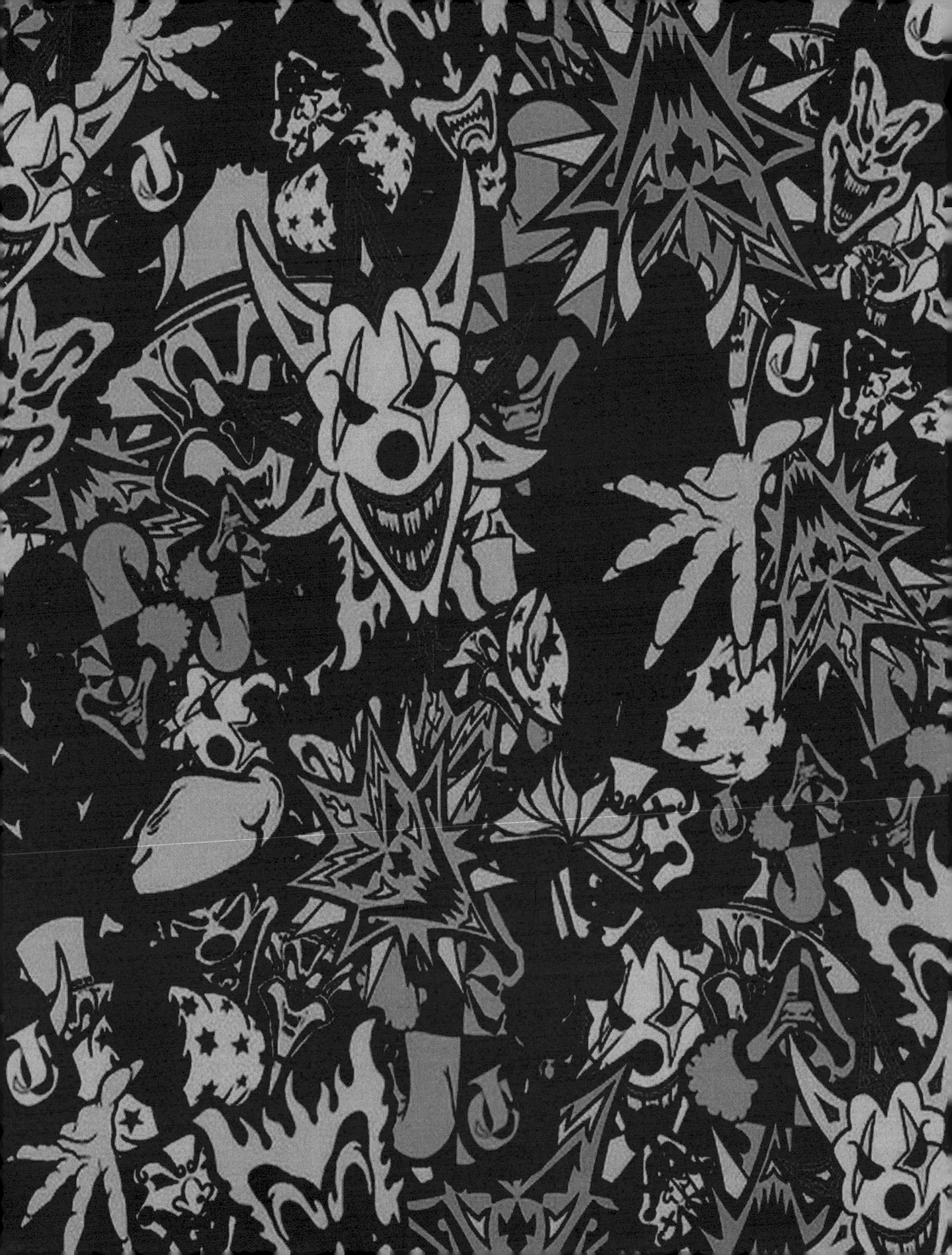

27956634R00061

Printed in Great Britain
by Amazon